STICKY SITUATIONS

Stories of Childhood
Adventures Abroad

By
Leigh Platt Rogers

ISBN 0-7414-1754-5

Published by:

PUBLISHING.COM

519 West Lancaster Avenue
Haverford, PA 19041-1413
Info@buybooksontheweb.com
www.buybooksontheweb.com
Toll-free (877) BUY BOOK
Local Phone (610) 520-2500
Fax (610) 519-0261

Printed in the United States of America

Printed on Recycled Paper

Published March 2004

Dedication

I would like to dedicate this book to my wonderful husband, Randy, for all his love, understanding and allowing me the opportunity to follow a dream.

Thank you, my darling.

All my love,

LLB

Table of Contents

Acknowledgements

I think that first and foremost, I must say that without my beloved husband, Randy, *Sticky Situations* would not have been possible. He gave me the opportunity to have the time and freedom I needed to write this book – along with some other stories I've been able to see published. Thank you, my love, not only for being there for me all the time, but for being my best friend as well.

I would also like to thank my much-loved parents, Jack and Paige, for their combined support as well as their collective contributions pulled from their memory banks. Without your help, I would have been at a loss. Delving into your perspectives about different experiences helped me with my own recollections. While my memories may not exactly match yours, let's remember who has the final say: *Moi* – L'Auteur!

To my sisters, Michelle and Diana, thank you for your constant belief in my ability to make writing a career. You will never know how much you helped me along. I took to heart all the support and encouragement you both gave me. You are both beautiful people. I also know that my nephew, Cody, was right there along with you two – cheering me on. What a great kid!

Next is my dearest Aunt Polly with whom I have commiserated endlessly about having "writers block" and the old "should I really include *that* story? No one's going to want to read about *that*." Thank you, "Evil Auntie" for your unconditional love, support and always being there for me. You are the best.

I want to acknowledge my mother-in-law, Doris, and sister-in-law, Karen, as well as my two nephews, Kyle and Collin. Words cannot express how much it meant to me when you asked about my writing and how it was going – and then to want to read the stories I had written. That is the highest form of praise. Most of all, though, Kyle inviting me to come to his school and talk to his peers about all my "overseas stories" was incredibly flattering. I was so surprised he had listened to my family tales so closely!

Janeene – my friend, pal, buddy – what would I ever do without you to talk to, to be able to be myself without fear of judgment or disdain, and to feel your unconditional support, love and constant empathy?! Thank you for just being *you* and I think you know I could have sprinkled some very "colorful" words throughout this book (since I used quite a few while writing it!) but I refrained out of respect for my audience.

Karen Chiao – family friend, writer, author – you have been an *incredible* mentor. You have been so wonderful and helpful to me. Thank you for your time, your suggestions, your advice and always being there to answer my endless questions. Your correspondence has meant a great, great deal to me.

To my dearest, long-time friend – Laurie – you have always been there for me and I am so grateful to have been blessed with such a wonderful friendship. Thank goodness we have been able to live through so much and still be around to tell it all! Thank you for graciously allowing me to share your stories as well as mine. You are much loved and much needed.

Finally, thank you to all my friends and Jazzercise buddies who are such a joy to me and who add immeasurable happiness and laughter to my life. Without your shoulders to cry on or your smiles to laugh with, I doubt I would have ever made it this far.

---Leigh Platt Rogers ☺

Introduction

I WAS a teenager when I found out what my father "really" did for a living. Having spent eleven years of my childhood growing up in three different countries overseas, you would think that I might have had some inkling that my father was a CIA agent. I honestly never considered it until we were in the middle of our last tour in Paris, France.

My father's true career was "discovered" because there was a man in the agency named Philip Agee who was a disgruntled ex-CIA employee. Agee left the agency bent on revenge for not being recognized as a genius. He published a book titled *CIA from A to Z* which revealed the names of undercover agents and other inside information. He was considered a traitor of the worst kind. Agee also helped newsmen at a Paris newspaper – *Liberation* – to analyze the U.S. Embassy telephone book. This was how the Parisian newspaper was able to name 44 people (they got 42 correct) who were CIA agents. My father's name was among the 42. Up until this time, my parents had told me that my father was a "Foreign Service Agent" and worked in the "Economics Department" at the American embassies in each of the countries we were assigned to.

After the newspaper article was published, I had students at school come up to me and ask me if my father worked for the CIA. Shocked, I denied it. I went and asked my father about it and he also told me that it was not true. Of course I believed my father. I mean – he was my *father*.

The way I finally discovered the truth was early one morning when we were in the car on the way out of town. I was on the verge of falling asleep but became wide awake when I overheard my mother asking my father whether our "phones were being tapped." I could not believe my ears! Did she just ask if our phones were *tapped*? My father answered, "Yes, I'm afraid so."

Then – in her exasperated voice – my mother asked, "Well, *when* will they be *untapped*?" My father told her he didn't know. That was all that was said.

When we arrived at our destination, I waited for a moment alone with my mother. I asked her why our phones were being tapped. My mother gave me a funny look and told me I would have to go and ask my father. So, I did. My father gave me a funny look too.

He sat me down and started talking. He got very serious and told me that he was sorry he had not told me about his "real" job sooner. At this moment, I realized my father was not kidding or joking around with me as he usually did. What he was saying was *very* important. He apologized for lying to me when I asked him earlier about his name being published in the newspaper. He was trying to keep his cover from being blown. He explained that he was a CIA agent and that the reason we had moved to all these different countries was because of his career. He told me that many of our family friends were also in the CIA.

My father painstakingly explained that he understood if his association with the CIA troubled me. He knew there was a great deal of political debate and difference of opinion over the effectiveness and viability of the agency as a whole. My father kept talking and talking and all the while, (he told me later) my eyes kept getting bigger and bigger. He said he could not figure out what I was thinking because I got my "Leigh-Look." My father calls it that because he says my face remains completely blank – no expression, no reaction – just big blue eyes staring back at you. Finally, he stopped – having apparently run out of anything more to say – and sat there looking at me. After a few moments of silence (my father says he was starting to get a little nervous), he asked, "So – what do you think?"

My father says I suddenly gave him a huge smile. "Dad," I said, "I'm *so* relieved!"

My father looked at me, puzzled. "You are?"

"Yeah!" I continued, "You know how we kept moving from country to country?" My father nodded. "Like, we lived in the United States and then had to leave and then come back and then leave again for another country?" My father kept nodding, wondering where I was going with this. "Well, you see – well – I thought – I thought that it was because *you couldn't keep a job.*"

My father stared at me blankly. I continued, "You know, like we kept having to move 'cause you were always getting fired from your jobs and that's why you and mom don't talk about what you do."

My father burst out laughing. Imagine having your teenage daughter thinking you were a bum who couldn't manage to keep a job. He got tears in his eyes he was laughing so hard. I joined him, of course. His laughter was irresistible. I also told him again that I was so happy that he had a *real* job! He was a spy! I was thrilled.

Then he told me I was going to have to keep my mouth shut and not reveal his true career to anyone. And he meant *anyone.* No one outside the immediate family could know. He was adamant that I had to understand how grave this was and how bad it would be if I told anyone. Although he did not go into great detail about the consequences, I understood that "grave" could mean something like a family member being kidnapped to get information from my father or something even worse. Of course, think about this – does anyone realize how hard it is for an energetic, thrilled, excited *teenager* to keep such incredible information to herself and not share it? But I did.

I can tell you all this now because my father is retired. And, while my father was an extremely successful agent, these stories are not about the spy business or his career. His adventures as an agent are his to tell. I wanted to write from

3

the viewpoint of a child experiencing life growing up overseas – complete with outlandish (but true!) stories.

When I talked to my father about my idea to write this book, he responded with his favorite quote delivered by Glenda Jackson in the movie, *"Hopscotch."* The movie is about a disgruntled CIA spy (played by Walter Matthau) who is seething about the stupidity of his boss and the fact that he has been reassigned to a desk job. Walter has decided to write his "memoirs" which is going to be a book about his 30 years with the CIA. He has decided to expose all the ineptitudes of various people from the CIA, FBI and the KGB. He is resolutely rolling paper into a typewriter when Glenda – who does not believe him at first – asks, "What are you really going to write about?"

Walter sits up straight and says proudly, "I am going to write the truth!"

And she responds, nodding benevolently, "Ah I see. It's going to be a work of *fiction.*"

I have a feeling – as I think about my family's reaction to this book – that there are probably some stories I am going to share that my parents *wish* were fiction. Perhaps they might even *wish* someone had not gone to all the trouble to write them down. However, this book is definitely not a work of fiction or fantasy. It is about the experience of living and growing up overseas in the 1960's and 1970's. It is about the exposure to different ways of life and to new languages. It is about learning to live in strange countries with remarkable people. It is about family and the challenges of childhood.

To describe my family as a whole is difficult, but in brief, I will say we are a mix of unique, intelligent, creative, witty, neurotic, controlling and compulsive individuals. My mother grew up in Upper State New York in a fairly affluent family. She was raised in a strict, puritan environment – although my grandmother did divorce and remarry which was not exactly socially acceptable during those times. My mother lived under the adage that children are to be 'seen and not heard.' My mother, Paige Gordon Platt, is an attractive woman with dark wavy hair, hazel eyes (which turn black when she's angry), long, lean legs and a shapely body. She dresses impeccably in well-fitted suits donned with matching scarves. My mother can wear jeans and a plain t-shirt and she looks like she is going to a party.

Jack, my father, "unusually" dressed up with my mother, Paige, at a party in Vienna, Austria – sometime around 1966 - 1967

My mother prides herself on her ability to work hard and make a difference. Teaching English as a second language while overseas was a challenge but one she enjoyed immensely. She has always had very high expectations of herself and these expectations have been bestowed upon the three children she raised. However, underneath her "perfect face" is an unsuspected impatience, irritation and the need for absolute control. My mother would shake her head and vehemently deny these allegations were she reading this over my shoulder – but I know this to be true from first-hand experience.

Always charming and the perfect hostess for guests and visitors, many people would never know that my mother has an amazing ability to stop someone in their tracks with a look. Only my sisters, my father and I have been privy to the power of my mother's barest glance. All I can tell you is when those stupendous dark eyes give you the withering "Look," you know you are in for it. Do not make a move. Do not say a thing. Do not ask a question. Just stop whatever you are doing. You won't have to wait long to understand what you did wrong. My mother will make sure you know *exactly* what she is not happy about. This is her underlying, tenacious and cleverly hidden intolerance of human ineptitude.

At first glance, my mother and father seem completely opposite of each other. My father, named John Cheney Platt III – but everyone calls him "Jack," was born in Texas and raised all over the world. My grandfather was in the Army and my father and his younger sister moved many times during their childhood. My father developed the survivalist's ability to quickly make new friends and adapt to different cultures, schools, languages and people. He has used this gift wisely in his career.

My father is a handsome man with thick, dark hair – which is now mostly salt and pepper. He has a hearty, infectious laugh. I can be in another room and just hearing my father's laugh makes me giggle. He has a slight "beer belly" which is no longer due to alcohol – he has been sober for many, many years. Instead, he satisfies his sweet tooth with "too much ice cream and candy," my mother says disparagingly.

My father is very different from my mother in appearance. His daily attire is a flannel shirt, jeans, cowboy boots and a hunting vest. His whole demeanor is of a person relaxed and without a care in the world. This face of tranquility and mellowness is deceptive. He doesn't miss a thing. When my sisters and I were little, my father corrected our misbehavior with what I call the "head-shot." With a quick smack to the back of the head (which did not hurt – it just startled you into stopping whatever you were doing), my father was able to quickly get our immediate attention.

Between my mother's "Look" and my father's instant form of reprimand, my sisters and I grew up as well-behaved and obedient children. I believe what has kept my parents together is their mutual respect for one another. My father genuinely adores my mother and desires her company more than any other. My mother feels safe and secure with my father and appreciates his joy of life.

As for myself, I find that I am a mix of both my mother and my father. I have my father's innate ability to be able to make conversation with just about anyone. I am social and love to be the center of attention. Around most people, I am cheerful, upbeat and funny. Only my husband and a few close friends know that there is a not-so-lovable side to me. I worry too much and agonize over even the smallest of decisions. I am too easily crushed by rejection and criticism. I have an obsessive-compulsive personality that can drive people around me crazy.

I have luckily inherited my mother's good looks and dark wavy hair. I am the only one in our family (dating back to my great-grandmother) with blue eyes. As a child, my hair was jet black and the contrast drew comments. "My, what amazing blue eyes," people would say.

I was not much of a talker when I was little. I spent more time watching and listening. I always had tons of energy. My mother used to tell me that I never walked. She said I went from crawling to running. It was as though I crawled until I had figured out how to run instead of waiting to learn to walk. She also told me it was the same thing about talking. She and my father were growing a little worried that there was something wrong with me because I refused to talk. Then one day, out of the blue, I started talking – and I spoke using full sentences. Again, she said it was though I waited until I was ready to be able to talk like an adult. No halfway stuff for me. It was either do it right or not at all. I suppose that is how I have lived most of my life.

My sisters, Michelle and Diana, are four years younger than me. They are identical twins and this phenomenon is always fascinating to people. They have beautiful, silky dark hair and luminous hazel eyes. Like me, they have "God's kisses" on their faces, the freckles making them look younger than they are.

As children, my mother refused to dress them alike because she wanted them to grow up and be themselves – strong and independent. My sisters were both very small for their age. They were happy children. They always had each other to play with if they found themselves alone. Growing up, they were cheerful, carefree and full of energy. They certainly kept all of us on the go with their numerous antics and adventures.

In 1966, our first tour was spent in Vienna, Austria where we lived for five years. I remember asking my mother once, long after we had returned to the United States, which country had been her favorite. She only briefly hesitated, reflecting, before telling me that she had the best memories and the most fun in Vienna. Vienna, she said, was a city of beauty and refinement; a place of history and culture; fascinating and entertaining. I don't remember Vienna the way my mother does, but I enjoy seeing the look of pleasure that comes over her face when she relates her stories and memories.

In 1971, we returned to the United States and lived in Rockville, Maryland for one year while my father waited for his next assignment. The tour we were sent on in 1972 was to Laos, a country located in Southeast Asia, where we lived in Vientiane, the capital of Laos. For two and a half years we were stationed in Vientiane. As in Austria, my mother adamantly refused to let us live on an American base. She felt very strongly that if we were going to live overseas, we were going to experience the culture and live among the people of the country. This was taking a risk in Laos, given the political turmoil in neighboring countries, but it was the one thing about which she stood firm.

Our final tour was in 1974 when we moved to France for three years. We lived in a small town outside Paris called Vaucresson. The change in climate from Laos to France was like night and day. Our bodies had become acclimated to the hot and humid weather year-round in Laos. The move to France in the beginning of fall was akin to arriving at the North Pole. It was between 60 – 70 degrees when we arrived, which sounds like comfortable temperatures to most. Given the fact that we were accustomed to living in a place that never got below 90 degrees, in Paris we were freezing all the time. That first year in France was the coldest I have ever experienced.

I wrote these stories with as much honesty and clarity that I could muster. I realize that my memories and recollections may be different from that of my parents and my sisters. Some of the writings may be somewhat embellished (what tale is complete without some "color?") and there may also be some "filler" (to smooth out the rough edges), but for the most part, this is "*my* truth."

And now – onto the adventures!

Vienna,
Austria

1966 – 1971

Vienna, Austria – late 1960's

A Rocky Beginning

THE LATE 1960's was the height of the Cold War[*]. There was political turmoil on many fronts. There were vigorous Communist Parties rising in Europe and growing domestic protest over the Vietnam War. As all of this was happening, the United States government was focusing efforts on the "containment" of the Soviets. My father had recently "graduated" from being trained as a CIA operative.

My father learned that Austria was a station in the midst of the Cold War geographically. My father already spoke German and had lived in Germany for 4 years while growing

---

[*] This is an overly simplified and brief explanation: the Cold War was a period of East-West competition, tension, and conflict short of full-scale war, characterized by mutual perceptions of hostile intention between military-political alliances. There was also competition for influence in the Third World, as well as the evolvement of a major superpower arms race.

up. He found a "slot" in Vienna for a street officer. It was exactly what he wanted to do and where he wanted to go.

We wound up staying in Austria for 5 years. This was somewhat unheard of for a first-tour officer. Most overseas assignments lasted only 2 to 3 years. My father loved the work and my mother adored Vienna. With a great place to live, interesting work, and surrounded by remarkable people, my father managed to successfully plot and scheme his way into finagling a longer stay.

When we first arrived in Vienna, my parents put me into an Austrian summer camp to "acclimatize" me to the Austrian culture. It was a day camp; my mother dropped me off in the mornings and picked me up in the afternoons. My parents thought it would be a good way for me to learn the language and meet some Austrian children. Even though I was only five years old at the time, I can still remember this place vividly. I *hated* it. My mother soon discovered that while the intention behind sending me to camp was good, it turned out to be a very bad idea.

I remember clinging to my mother's neck and crying, begging her not to leave me as she carried me to the door. To me, this camp was a horrible place. All I saw was a large brown building that looked like a prison. Inside were picnic tables with long benches where we ate our lunch. Behind the building was a large dirt yard where the children played soccer. The children refused to let me play in any of their games.

Shooed outside by the camp counselor, I sat in the dirt with my back against the fence and watched the others run around, laughing and talking in a language that sounded like gibberish to me. Even the food we ate was strange. Every day for lunch we were served watery chicken noodle soup with brown bread. For a snack we had a sugar cookie and a cup of orange juice that tasted like a mix between Tang and regular orange juice. No one spoke to me. All the children ignored me. And it never got any better.

Every day I lived for the moment when my mother would show up to take me home. I would beg her not to make me go back there. My mother thought that over a period of time I would adjust and find that I liked the camp, but that never happened. I cried every time I saw where we were going. I screamed for my mother when she drove away. I felt lost, alone and abandoned. It was an awful experience that I have never forgotten. My mother finally gave up and took me out of the camp, to my immense relief.

If you were to ask my mother about this place, she would most likely get a bemused look on her face. She would tell you that she could not understand why I displayed such a vehement dislike of the camp. I can hear her response in my head as clear as a bell. She would say (in her proper voice and in her proper way), "It was such a *quaint* little place. It was built like a log cabin with a beautifully landscaped front yard. The camp owner was a sweet older woman who was very kind and loved children. And she even spoke English nicely." Then my mother would sigh, "I never really understood why Leigh hated that place so much."

The Apartment

IN VIENNA, the first place we moved into was a large apartment. We lived on the third floor. The building itself did not look like an apartment building. Rather, it looked like an enormous mansion. It was designed in an elegant European fashion with walls made of grey stone, long windows and small towers at the top. There was a short path leading from the gated entrance to the front steps which were what I call "Cinderella steps." They were wide at the bottom and as you walked up, the steps narrowed until you reached the front door.

While it was a beautiful apartment building, there was one memorable drawback: The Dog. The landlady who resided on the first floor owned a big, black Labrador. The dog was *massive* and looked more like a large beast than a dog. His favorite place of rest was the front steps and when he was stretched out, he easily covered the entire landing in front of the door.

If someone approached (unless it was his beloved owner), he would slowly raise his head, lazily stare at the intruder and then a low rumbling growl would begin. His upper lip would slowly lift up just enough to show some large, sharp teeth. The landlady assured us that the dog would not harm us, but I did not believe her. I would cower and tremble as I climbed the steps, trying to slip silently around the immense creature as it lay with one eye closed, the other following my every move. The low, nonstop rumbling would continue from deep within its throat.

Once I reached the door, I would quickly pull it open and leap inside, slamming the door behind me. Each time I breathed a sigh of relief that I was still alive. The good days were when I would descend the stairs from our apartment and there was no sign of the "Black Monster." Those were celebratory moments, although they were few and far between.

Our apartment was quite large with high ceilings and a beautifully designed interior. The wooden floors were a polished golden color. The living room and dining room were very stylish with tall glass doors separating the rooms. I had my own room located near the back of the long apartment. I was close to the narrow kitchen, which had a very small breakfast nook. The master bedroom where my parents slept was large and had dark paneling. This gave the room a cozy feeling despite its size.

As for where my sisters slept, my mother decided to put them and their cribs in a tiny room, which was built to be more of a closet than a bedroom. This bedroom was so narrow that the cribs could only fit if placed head-to-head vertically. You could access the twins "bedroom" through the hall door, but there were also double doors that opened into another huge open room. This large room was officially designated as the twin's playroom. It, too, had a beautiful, polished wooden floor and tall windows, which lit up the room nicely. There was no furniture in this room except for numerous bookshelves that lined the walls. These were filled with toys, books and stuffed animals. My parents had purchased, built and painted the bookshelves bright colors – blue, green, red, yellow.

One of my nightly chores was to assist with cleaning up the playroom (which was destroyed by the twins during the day). This meant putting all items back in the bookshelves and collecting the numerous building blocks which were spread all over the room. With the assistance of my creative and industrious father, we would build huge elaborate castles with the blocks. Together we made tall towers, built high walls and even designed complex mazes. This chore was always much more fun when my father helped me.

The big moment was in the morning when my mother got up to let the "little monsters" (as she called them) out of their room. We could always tell when the twins were awake because they made so much noise. They never cried. They were usually laughing and yelling with delight. They had learned early on how to jump up and down in their cribs and rock them back and forth until the heads of the crib would bash together. This set off peals of laughter. Again they would jump and jump, yelling with glee, until the next big bang happened. My mother always said it was a wonder those cribs lasted as long as they did. As soon as my mother or father went into the room, Michelle and Diana would shout to be picked up and then immediately wanted to get down. Impatiently, my sisters would wait for the double doors to be opened (which were locked at night) that led to the playroom.

As soon as those doors were opened, Michelle and Diana would rush into the room, overjoyed at the sight of the intricate castles and mazes and tunnels. Instantly they would smash everything we had carefully built the night before in less than a minute. Kicking their tiny legs and swinging their little arms, they danced with delight watching the blocks tumbling down. The crashing and banging echoed through the apartment. When every single building block had been successfully toppled, all towers demolished and the mazes eliminated, my sisters – exalted and satiated – would then sit contentedly and begin playing. In less than a minute, our painstaking castle-creations had been destroyed. I would sigh at the sight, knowing I would have to resume my nightly chore of creating another fantasyland for my sisters.

One time Michelle and Diana were given little goose-down pillows as a gift. My mother made the mistake of letting the twins sleep with their new pillows. Quite early the very next morning, the familiar sounds of laughter could be heard from my sisters' room. I heard someone open the door to the twins' room. Then I heard a gasp of horror and the door to the room was slammed shut.

Groggy, I went out into the hall and peered at my mother who was facing the closed door with her hand over her mouth. She had a look of shock on her face. I came up beside her and asked her what was wrong. She could not speak, merely gestured for me to open the door. As soon as I did, I was appalled. The room was covered – literally *covered* in goose feathers. It was like it was snowing in the room. In the midst of the flying feathers were my sisters, jumping up and down, grabbing at the feathers with one hand and waving their torn pillowcases in the other. Apparently they had started a pillow fight and the small pillows were not up to the test.

My mother is sure it did not take long for those pillowcases to burst open, unleashing a snowstorm of goose feathers over my leaping, cheering sisters. What a day that was. My mother was amazed that these tiny little pillows had so many feathers in them. It took all day to clean them up. Feathers were still being found months later, popping up from out of nowhere.

The playroom had tall windows that were mid-room to ceiling level and had iron rods on the outside, presumably to prevent anyone from falling out. The windows faced the sidewalk below where people walked by, perhaps on their way to the beautiful park located across the street from our building. One warm summer day I was in the kitchen, looking out the window – which also faced the street – when I noticed a crowd of people gathering in front of the gate. They were pointing up at my sisters' playroom and gesturing among themselves. Suddenly, I saw a doll followed by a wooden block fly out of the window to the ground below. I was initially amused as I puzzled for a moment about what was happening until I saw more toys flying through the air. Realizing the source, I called for my mother and we rushed to the playroom.

When we got there, we saw both my sisters had actually climbed up on the iron bars through the open window and were tossing out whatever item was nearby, laughing with glee. My mother leapt forward, plucked the Michelle off the bars and handed her to me. The laughter instantly turned into screams of protest. Then she tried to grab Diana who quickly climbed higher like a little monkey.

After a few minutes of wrangling with the protesting, screaming twin, my mother was able to get Diana down. Below we could hear the crowd voicing exclamations and laughter. Meanwhile, I tried to find something to divert the twins' attention. After things were calm and they were quietly playing, I went down and collected all the toys and other items that had been scattered on the ground by my gleeful siblings – just another adventurous day.

"Perfect" Big Sister

OF COURSE, I cannot say that I was the perfect older sister. I recall one time when my sisters were still "babies" and I was playing with them in the living room. To amuse myself, I went and got a broom from the kitchen pantry and decided to act like I was a witch. Everything was fine for a few minutes until disaster struck. I swung the broom too close to the glass doors that separated the dining room and living room and – *SMASH* – down crashed an entire glass panel from one of the doors. Glass shattered and flew everywhere.

I stood completely frozen in shock. I knew I was in *big trouble*. My sisters were sitting on the floor on the opposite side of the room so they were not injured, but I was scared to death of facing my mother. As soon as I got my senses back, I decided I had to find some kind of logical explanation that my mother would believe. I could hear my mother walking down the hall. I swiftly ran over to my sisters, put the broom across their tiny laps and then rushed over to sit on the sofa, trying not to look guilty.

When my mother walked in, this was what she saw: a broken door panel, glass all over the floor and me on the sofa looking terrified. She also saw the twins with a heavy broom on their laps, staring at my mother with big eyes. What I forgot to consider in my search for a "way out," was the fact that neither of my sisters could have lifted that broom, much less swing it around and break a glass panel.

My mother stood there, hands on her hips, and gave me that, *'Don't-even-try-and-convince-me-your-sisters-did-this'* look. I hung my head, caught. Not only had I been careless enough to bring a broom into the living room, where playing was forbidden, but I also tried to place the blame on "the babies." My mother explained that it would have been much better to come forward, admit my guilt and learn from the consequences. Because I tried to plead not guilty and blame my sisters, I was punished a little more harshly. I was grounded for two weeks (meaning *no* trips to the park!) and given "dish-duty" which meant I had to help clean up after dinner. I learned a lesson that day.

There was another time when I proved once again to my mother that I was not the "perfect" child she thought me to be. My mother was not home and Margaret (alias "Margit"), our nanny, was taking care of making dinner in the kitchen. I have no idea what I was angry about. I probably wanted a cookie and Margit said no since dinner would soon be on the table or something equally silly.

I do remember that I was lying on my stomach on the floor in the hall just outside the kitchen and I was throwing a *major* temper tantrum. Margit was completely ignoring me so I am sure it was not the first time I had done this with her. I recall that I was kicking my legs up in the air behind me and thrashing my arms around and screaming like a maniac when my mother walked in the door. She had never seen me throw a temper tantrum before. She stood there in complete shock while I wailed on and on until suddenly I sensed someone watching and turned to see my mother standing there. I was instantly horrified and froze where I was. Seeing the look on my mother's face was enough to send anyone into a catatonic state. Before she could say anything, I jumped up and ran to my room.

My mother, after getting over the initial shock of seeing her beautiful, dutiful and serene daughter metamorphosed into a wild, screaming beast, turned and marched into my room. What ensued was a rather colorful lecture – one that I prefer not to share but I will say it was very effective. I never had another temper tantrum without first checking to see where my mother was and when she would be home.

George and Harold

SINCE WE were living in an apartment, my mother would not allow us to have any pets. She finally, however, caved in after my begging began to drive her crazy. She let me get two hamsters: George and Harold.

At first George and Harold were very small and cute, but it seemed that in no time at all, they got big and fat. Hamsters are not exactly the most playful of animals. For a 6-year old, it got rather boring just watching them sleep and eat in their cage. They even stopped using the rotating wheel we bought specially for them.

I tried taking the hamsters down to the small yard on the side of the apartment where there was a small grassy area and some trees. I would let George and Harold out of their cage and watch carefully for any sign of activity, but most of the time they just sat there looking around with big eyes, tentatively sniffing the grass. I'd even try and give them a push but neither of them would budge.

Finally, I decided that drastic measures were called for to enliven this sorry twosome. In my bedroom, I covered the floor with blankets and pillows. Then I got out "The

Machine." It was a portable record player that I had gotten for my birthday. I chose George to start with. I lifted him out of his cage and placed him on the record player's turntable.

At first, I merely turned the record on the turntable very slowly to test the waters. George held on and did not move.

So, I turned the record player on and placed the lever on 33 – the slowest setting. I placed the record needle on the record and it started playing. George was a bit heavy so it slowed the record down – the song sounded like it was being sung in slow motion. I wondered how long George would be able to stay on because he was looking quite terrified and his little claws were digging into the record.

After about two turns, he started to slowly slide toward the record's edge – his little back legs were scrambling to keep him still but it wasn't working. Fascinated, I watched as he started sliding faster and faster – the scratching sounds getting more and more desperate – until he fell off the record and landed on a pillow. I picked him up and looked him over – he was fine although his heart seemed to be beating a bit fast.

I looked at Harold who was asleep in the cage. It was time to get him up for his turn. I put the trembling George in the cage and picked up Harold who looked at me sleepily. "It's your turn!" I sang and put him on the spinning record. I guess he did not have time to balance himself because he flew off after one turn! Like George, he was a bit dazed but okay.

I was having so much fun, I called my sisters to come and see what I was doing. They came running in (they were about two years old). I showed them my new activity, which made them both giggle and laugh. Poor Harold. He was doomed to be the experimental hamster. After a few turns and a few falls off the record, I decided it was time for something more exciting.

I told my sisters to watch but to also be careful because things might get a little crazy. They clapped their hands and cheered. I took a deep breath and looked at Harold. "Come on, buddy," I said, "Hang in there because, dude, you are going for a *ride!*" I pushed the notch on the record player up to 45 – the fastest setting. The record started turning at great speed – the music sounded awful but I didn't care. I got Harold ready and held him over the spinning record and yelled, "Okay everyone! Here we go!!"

I dropped Harold and in a split second he was in the air, flying across the room at incredible speed. We watched in awe as he arced high in the air, eyes bulging and feet spread out wide until he landed with a loud 'POOF' in one of the pillows in the far corner. "Oh my gosh!" I shouted with glee. "That was cool!" I ran over to check on him. He was shaking all over and his heartbeat was like a booming drum.

Suddenly there was my father in the doorway. I clutched Harold to my chest in a protective manner. "Hi – uh – hi Dad."

He cleared his throat and said, "Just what is going on in here and why is that music sounding so terrible?"

"Oh," I replied, "Nothing, really. We were just playing."

"Playing what?"

I was about to try and downplay the situation when the twins piped up. In unison they excitedly explained to my father *exactly* what I was showing them. He rolled his eyes but also laughed and said, "Well, now, why don't you just show me?"

So, I did. My father cracked up and just as the four of us were all whooping it up about how funny Harold looked flying through the air, my mother appeared in the doorway. She was frowning. "And just what is going on in here?" she asked. Silently we all looked at her with big eyes.

"Nothing?" I tentatively answered.

"Hmmm," she nodded. "Okay – what are you four up to?"

Reluctantly I turned and sent Harold flying through the air one last time. My mother smothered a laugh and said, "Oh my goodness! Poor, *poor* Harold. Leigh – ," she held my eyes with hers, "You mustn't do that to the poor hamster. The record player is for playing records – not for flying your hamsters through the air." I could see she was trying not to smile so I knew I wasn't in bad trouble – but I also knew she was right. If you have a pet, you need to treat it right.

I sighed as everyone filed out of my room. I hugged Harold, thanked him for his participation and put him back in the cage. He immediately went up to George and they sniffed each other, turned their backs on me and buried themselves in the sawdust. I think they were a bit upset. I refrained from torturing them with the record player trick again – but I chuckle to this day when I think about flying hamsters. George and Harold were very entertaining that day.

Turken Schanz Park

JUST ACROSS the street from our apartment in Vienna was a beautiful park called Turken Schanz Park (pronounced 'turk-in-shawnz'). This park was renowned for its green lawns, gorgeous oak trees and the beautiful lake around which the park was located. The people of Vienna were passionate about keeping their city parks immaculate. Visitors to the park revered the quiet tranquility and peacefulness. They came to walk slowly through the beautiful surroundings and to admire the lovely grounds and serene lake where ducks and swans lazily floated.

We loved going to the park which had a playground area equipped with a large sandbox, swings and slides. On one of our "park days," my mother took the three of us to the playground. I immediately ran off to play on the slides while my mother put both twins in the sandbox, each with their own shovel and bucket. The sandbox was shaped in a round circle with some "S" curves and it was very large. The twins were still very young – about 18 months old – and they were content to sit in the warm sand and play. The park was quite crowded with lots of young Austrian children in the sandbox. Their mothers sat on park benches close by, talking and keeping an eye on their children. My mother was a stranger and an American so she sat alone while the other mothers socialized.

Things were quiet for a little while. My mother was reading a book she brought to pass the time when something caught her eye. A little Austrian boy who was probably somewhere around 2 or 3 years old, got up from his spot in the sandbox. He walked over to where Michelle was contentedly playing with her shovel and bucket. This boy, a sturdy, pudgy thing, watched Michelle and the shovel for a minute before making a decision. He suddenly bent down and wrenched the shovel away from Michelle. He rocked back on his heels, looked at the shovel with a great deal of satisfaction, then walked back to where he'd been playing and sat down. Shocked and dismayed, Michelle looked at her empty hand and started to cry. Diana, who was sitting directly across from Michelle, had observed the theft. For a brief moment she just sat there and watched her sister sob. My mother, startled by the boy's actions scanned the group of Austrian women to see if the boy's mother had witnessed the incident. Seeing no one moving, she began to get up but Diana beat her to it.

With a look of fierce determination and fury, Diana got up with her shovel gripped tightly in her tiny hand. She marched over to the boy (who was at least two times her size and probably three times her weight) and looked down at him for a moment while he played with *her sister's* shovel. Then Diana raised her shovel high above her head and before my mother could move or shout, down came Diana's blue shovel. She whacked the boy hard on the head with a loud *CRACK!* The boy – a look of pain and shock on his face – turned toward his tormentor. When he saw who it was, he screamed at the top of his lungs, dropped the shovel and grabbed his head with both hands. Diana, seeing her sister's shovel was free, calmly reached down, took the shovel and marched back to her sister, who had watched this episode with big eyes, all tears forgotten. With a look of pure vindication on her face, Diana plumped back down in the sand and returned the stolen shovel to its rightful owner.

Meanwhile, now that the tables had turned and her boy was "the victim," the Austrian mother was incensed. She jumped up, gathered up her boy who was still screaming and started yelling at my mother about Diana. My mother, not yet able to speak anything more than broken German, pointed at the boy and said, "Hey, your kid started it."

The Austrian mother, a large, well-fed housewife, picked up her screaming boy and hugged him tightly to her sizable chest. A stream of incomprehensible German poured from her mouth while she pointed an accusatory finger at Diana. Finally, my mother got fed up and said, "Lady, *get over* it."

More of the Austrian mothers got up, supporting the boy's mother, and began heatedly yammering at my mother. Sensing that she was now in enemy territory, my mother called for me (I had no idea all this exciting stuff was happening 10 feet away!) and told me to grab one of the babies while she grabbed the other.

As we rapidly left the park, my mother pushed the stroller faster and faster until I was running to keep up. I breathlessly asked my mother why we had to leave so soon. She told me, "Michelle had her shovel taken by a bully and now the bully has a hurt head." We hurried through the park while I puzzled about how taking a shovel meant someone had a hurt head, but one look at my mother's face said to drop it. It was much later that I got the full story about my brave sister and the lengths she would go to protect her twin sister.

From the time we moved into the apartment, my mother worried about the driving tactics of the Austrian people. To get to the park from our apartment, we had to cross a street of 4 lanes where people drove their cars like they were still on the Autobahn[*]. The other problem was that our nanny, Margit, was a good-looking young woman but she absolutely refused to wear her glasses outside of the apartment. She felt the glasses were horribly unattractive. So, on the days when we were to go to the park, my mother would watch in great trepidation while the four of us got ready to go.

After leaving the apartment, we would walk down the sidewalk to the curb. Standing on the edge of the massively wide street with cars whizzing by, Margit would tightly hold my hand and tell me to watch for an opening in the traffic so we could cross without danger. Margit would peer right and left, but was unable to make out anything with her blurred eyesight. She relied on me to find the perfect moment to

---

[*] The Autobahn is a high-speed highway system legendary for apparently having no speed limits. It is an extensive network of freeways located in Germany that can usually provide a driver with a speedy route from city to city.

move. Upstairs in the apartment, my mother would watch these proceedings with her heart standing still – routing for the party of four to succeed in braving the screaming metal of large, brutal BMW's and Peugeots.

Meanwhile, down below, I would look rapidly back and forth until I was sure there was a space of time available to cross the mighty street. At that moment, I would tell Margit that it was all clear and we could cross. Margit would push the stroller and I would hurry along beside her, all the while glancing up and down the street.

As my mother will swear to this day, every single time we started out across that street, about halfway to the other side, she would see me jump up and down and scream something at Margit. Margit would suddenly begin pushing the stroller with all her might, quickly breaking into a run. Meanwhile, I had already raced across the rest of the street. While Margit struggled with the stroller, I could be seen safely on the other sidewalk, yelling for her to "Go! Go! Go!" Margit would subsequently scold me for letting her cross when there were cars coming and I would always reply that when we started, there were none. I wonder now if she ever really believed me.

Once in the park, we always had a good time. We would let the twins out of the stroller (they were firmly strapped in for a reason) and they loved running up and down the walkways and onto the smooth, manicured grass. Margit would run after them, scolding the whole time about not touching the grass. Standing, walking or doing *anything* to the beautifully landscaped green lawns was strictly forbidden in the park.

The Tenacity of a Toddler

MOST OF our trips to the park were uneventful. However, I do remember one particular day. As usual, Margit was out of breath and I was running ahead to get to the play area. She let the twins out of the stroller and away they flew – in opposite directions. Maybe they were just getting faster or perhaps smarter, but this time she was not able to catch either one as they zoomed past. She screamed at me to *come back!* I must have heard something in her voice (it's called panic) because I stopped cold and turned back. I easily caught Michelle who was running in my direction, but up ahead I saw disaster looming. Margit had not been able to catch up with Diana who had swerved off toward the lake and was rapidly approaching the water.

I ran as fast as my legs could carry me, dragging my little sister along behind me. I saw Margit hesitate at the edge of the grass where a few people had stopped and were gawking at the sight before them. I caught up to Margit in time to see that Diana had not only reached the lakeshore, but was *in* the lake and was grinning from ear to ear. As I shot past Margit, I dropped off Michelle. I could hear Diana laughing and yelling, "Birdy! I gotta birdy!"

Diana had somehow actually managed to catch a large duck. She had her tiny hands around its neck and the bird – probably traumatized for the rest of its life – was squawking and frantically flapping its wings. It is almost inexplicable how Diana, as tiny as she was, held onto this duck, which was bigger than she was. But hang on she did and then began manhandling the poor, distraught thing back to shore, no doubt to give it to her sister who was jumping up and down yelling about wanting a "birdy" too!

Margit had Michelle firmly by the hand and was apologizing to the growing group of park visitors who were telling her that this child was doing something terribly wrong (like she hadn't already figured that out). Both Margit and I were also yelling "No! Diana, let the duck GO! Let it *GO!*" I can still remember the look of determination and stubbornness that was on Diana's face. There was no way she was giving up this "birdy." Finally, the duck got the upper hand and just as Diana had almost strangled the thing on her way onto the grass, it got away and half-flew, half stumbled back onto the lake with a horrified, tortured look on its face. Soaking wet, covered in mud and her prize gone, Diana wailed in fury. Her sister Michelle, held in an iron grip by Margit, sobbed in unison with her sister's dissatisfaction. I ran over, grabbed Diana – who was terribly angry – and wrestled her to the walkway.

Margit, fully relieved that all four of us were back on cement, ignored the citizens who were babbling on about these unruly children. She cleaned Diana's face and tried to calm down the sobbing siblings. As for me, I knew I wasn't going to get my day on the swings and slides.

My sinking stomach told me we'd be going home and someone was going to have to explain to my mother why Diana was covered in mud and why both twins had tear-streaked faces. I also have to admit that I felt something that I could not have verbalized at my age. I felt admiration for Diana's determination and single-mindedness. She knew what she wanted and by golly, she went and got it.

Home we went and sure enough, my mother met us at the door with a concerned frown on her face. As Margit tried to describe what happened, I could see my mother was fighting a smile that was threatening to take control. She tried to be firm with Diana and Michelle and explain the rules of the park (once again), but it was obvious she was about to burst out laughing. Besides, the twins had long forgotten the incident and were both squirming and struggling to get to their playroom. My mother gave up and let them go.

Later that night, when I was in bed, I could just make out my mother telling my father about Diana's "adventure" in the park and heard my father's infectious laughter. If I had ventured out to the dining room, I am sure I would have seen my parents trying to stop each other from laughing too loudly, tears in their eyes and hands over their mouths.

The Bakery

THERE WAS another interesting adventure that occurred when my sisters were still quite young. One day, Margit decided to take the twins with her while doing some errands and shopping. One of the stores she stopped at was a bakery. Bakeries in Europe are wondrous stores with windows filled with luscious cakes and candies. The window displays are usually meticulously put together to give a colorful and tantalizing vision of all the delicious items that can be found inside. The Viennese, in particular, are very proud of their artistry in product displays.

On this particular day, when Margit and the twins arrived at the bakery, it was rather crowded. Margit had to wait a few minutes to put in her order. Absentmindedly, she dropped the twins' hands while she searched in her purse for her wallet. Suddenly free, Michelle and Diana wasted no time.

A few seconds later, Margit looked around for Michelle and Diana but they were gone. She quickly searched the store with her eyes, and was about to call their names when she realized there was something going on behind her outside the shop. There was a crowd of people standing in front of the window pointing and gasping in astonishment. With growing apprehension, Margit rushed out to the front of the store with the owner of the shop right behind her. They both stopped still with shock at the sight before them.

There in the window, grinning from ear to ear, were the twins and they were shoveling every beautifully decorated delicatessen they could get their little hands on into their mouths. Their faces, hands and clothes were *covered* in chocolate and icing. The store display was absolutely destroyed.

With her characteristic *"Eeeeeeeeee!"* Margit rushed back into the store and grabbed the twins from the window.

Michelle and Diana wailed in frustration and began to cry – the tears making tracks down their chocolate-covered cheeks. The Viennese people were now all talking and gesturing toward the threesome as Margit tried to graciously depart from the shop as quickly as possible. The owner, who was understandably very upset, was practically pushing her and the twins from the shop, stammering and yelling at them to get out. Margit turned and tried to apologize, even offering to pay for the damage, but the owner just wanted them all out, out *OUT*!

When she got home to inform my mother that they would not be doing any shopping at the local bakery anymore, my mother was both horrified and amused at the sight of my sisters. She was also amazed at the agility, quickness and boldness of these two. No wonder she called them "Double Trouble." Once again, letting them go for just a moment could mean a possible disaster.

The House on the Cul-de-Sac

AFTER THE apartment, we moved to a house. It was located down a gravel road, off a main street, in a cul-de-sac. I loved this house. My bedroom was upstairs; my parents and sisters were downstairs so I felt I had lots of privacy. The living room was also upstairs so I always got the first peek on Christmas morning. I was allowed to look but not touch.

There is something incredibly wonderful about Christmas morning when it's still dark and everyone is asleep. I loved to start the magic by plugging in the Christmas tree lights and letting the smell of pine fill my senses. And, of course, gasping at the mountain of gifts that had been left by Santa Claus! By that time I would be so excited, I would rush down to my sisters' rooms and wake them up.

The three of us would open our stockings, look at our little gifts and eat the tangerines that Santa had left. Giggling and laughing, we could hardly wait for our parents to get up. I now know that my mother and father were, of course, awake but they loved to make us wait. After an eternity, they would slowly dress and make their way upstairs to get their coffee. Then, *finally*, we were allowed to open gifts.

We had a cat named Blackie who was all black except for a white spot on her chest. She got pregnant and my mother explained to the three of us that Blackie was going to have kittens. My mother made a place in the closet in the laundry room for Blackie to give birth. She tried to get Blackie accustomed to going there. My mother discovered, however, that there was someone else in the house who was as determined and stubborn as she.

One afternoon, Diana came running, crying to my mother that there were "mouses" in her bed. My mother did not understand what she meant until Diana told her that Blackie was "licking the mouses." Sure enough, instead of the nice box in the closet with the clean, fluffy towels, Blackie had ignored my mother's efforts at directing the birthplace of her litter and chose instead to have the "mouses" in Diana's bed. The newborn kittens did indeed look like tiny little mice. My mother assured the twins that they would turn into kittens. It was an amazing thing to watch the six kittens grow. Eventually we had to give them away, which just about broke my heart.

The cul-de-sac that we lived on had two other houses occupied by Austrian families. One of the families had a young boy who was a little older than me – around 10 or 11 years old. He was the neighborhood bully. If I was riding my bike, he would run after me and push me off. He also delighted in harassing my sisters.

One day, though, the tables turned on him. Diana came running up to my mother who was in the laundry room doing some ironing. Diana was in a rage and told my mother that the Austrian boy had thrown rocks at her and Michelle. My mother, distracted, murmured something comforting to my sister and patted her on the head. When her hand came away, it felt wet. She glanced down and gasped. Her hand was covered in blood, as was my sister's head. The bully had not only thrown rocks, but also managed to launch a large one that had cracked Diana's skull!

Alarmed, my mother rushed to take Diana to the medical clinic. On her way out to the car, the boy's mother confronted her. The woman was like a large, bellowing cow, yelling at my mother and pointing at Diana in an accusatory manner. She had her son locked under one arm, clutching him tightly to her immense bosom. Apparently, the counter attack Diana and Michelle had unleashed in a fury had taken him completely off guard. Even while Diana's head was oozing blood, the twins had managed to return such a tremendous volley of rocks and gravel, that the "bully" had no option but to run home like a coward. He had sustained some minor injuries – a few scratches and bruises. My mother almost laughed as she watched him cower from the twins. Even with a cracked skull, Diana had not shed one tear.

My mother calmly told the woman in broken German that her son had started this whole mess. She showed the woman Diana's bleeding skull and told her that the wound was serious and needed immediate medical attention. The Austrian mother continued her tirade whereupon my mother turned her back, told both twins to get in the car and ignored the now red-faced, screeching neighbor. After that incident, the boy never bothered any of us again.

There was another incident I remember well that happened while we lived at this house. The big push for seatbelt safety had not yet evolved. If we were only going to drive a short distance, my mother would let the twins stand up in the backseat and hold onto the front seat headrests. My mother would have one twin behind her and I would have the other behind me. They would laugh and bounce up and down as the wind blew back their hair. I am sure it felt a little like flying. We would tell them to hold on tight and normally there was never a problem – until one frightening day.

We had just left the cul-de-sac. My mother turned onto the main road, made a quick right turn and headed down the street. After about 5 seconds, Diana – who was holding onto my passenger seat headrest – said something to me. I turned to look at her and she had a puzzled look on her face. I asked her what she said and she repeated, "Michelle go bye-bye?" I looked for Michelle who should have been behind my mother, but there was no little girl hanging on and grinning. There was just a slightly open car door.

I opened my mouth to say something to my mother but she had already taken it all in and screeched the car to a dead stop. Panicked, she ran up the street where, sure enough, there was Michelle all crumpled up in the middle of the road. She could have easily been killed by another car. She was so small people would not have seen her until they were right on top of her. Thankfully, no cars had come by and Michelle was breathing although unconscious.

Unbelievably, my mother saw that directly across from where Michelle had fallen out, there was a young man (my mother describes him as a "hippy"), who was sitting on a bench. He had not made one move to help my sister. Although she was enraged by his lack of compassion for a young child, my mother had no time for confrontation. She could not believe that someone would just sit there and not try to help a child in trouble.

We rushed to get Michelle some medical care. The doctor looked her over and said she was just fine except for a few bruises. After that, the twins were strapped into the car seats, much to their dislike, but my mother turned a deaf ear to their dissatisfaction with the seating arrangements. When I recall that incident, I don't remember that I felt any fear – probably because my mother was with me. I am quite sure the terror my mother must have experienced at that moment is not a feeling that I would ever want to share.

Because I was a constant caretaker for my sisters, particularly in their younger years, most of my early memories are about them and the situations they were always falling into. But there is one recollection I have of my father and the large pool that we had in the backyard. The pool was not heated and the water was extremely cold – like "liquid ice" is how I remember it.

Every morning I would accompany my father down to the pool and watch as, dressed in only his swimming trunks, he would dive into the frigid water and swim a few laps. I would shiver with admiration because I knew how cold the water was. He would get out of the pool, soaking wet and all red from the cold, and dry off with a towel telling me that this was the best way to clear his head. If it had been anyone other than my father I would have thought they were crazy, but my father was (and always will be) my hero.

After the swim, he would change for work. Then we would have breakfast together while my mother joined us with her coffee. The twins, of course, were still in highchairs and – as usual – their breakfast would not only be in their mouths, but also all over the highchair, the floor, and in their hair. They loved mealtime.

The American School of Vienna

I STARTED Kindergarten at the American School of Vienna. It was a large facility that accommodated students from Kindergarten through the 12th grade. I remember the halls were brightly painted with posters and pictures all over the walls. I loved school and excelled as a student. I don't have very many memories associated with my first few years there, except the time when my father was in a play at the school.

My father was a member of the "Embassy Players." This was a group of people that got together to put on plays to raise money for student scholarships. The play performed at my school was *The Odd Couple.* My father played the role of Oscar, which he fit perfectly. I recall that I was busting with pride when I saw the show and it was a big hit with the audience. My father was terrific.

The best scene was when Felix got so upset with Oscar that he threw a whole pot of spaghetti noodles against the wall. Oscar (my father) looked very calmly at the noodles stuck to the wall and, to Felix's horror, got up and ate one of the noodles. Then he said to Felix, "Hey, I think these are done. Let's eat!" That really cracked the audience up.

One of my more frightening memories of Vienna was when my sisters started Kindergarten and I was in the 3rd grade. Almost all the students rode buses to and from school. Each bus was assigned a number and every student was supposed to remember their bus number. Because of the number of students, sometimes finding the right bus was difficult. The buses were also supposed to line up in numerical order but that often did not happen.

I had been going to this school for the past 4 years so I knew what to do, but I was nervous that I would not be able to find my sisters before the our bus left. To make matters worse, the first day of school was greeted with a torrential rainstorm that lasted all day.

At the end of the day, by the time I got out to where the buses were lined up, students and teachers were rushing here and there, each person trying to board their bus without getting drenched. I searched desperately for my sisters, looking for the identical raincoats my mother had made them wear so they would be easier to find. My desperation became terror that they had boarded the wrong bus or that they were lost.

Soon my face was drenched not only with the rain, but with my own panicky tears. The heavy weight of responsibility I felt was overwhelming. I looked in vain for a teacher or anyone to help me but the buses were already starting to leave! And then, I saw the two of them, huddled together at the far end of the line of buses. They were obviously terrified and crying, clutching at each other for comfort. Immense relief flooded my body and I raced toward them with open arms.

They reached for me, sobbing my name over and over. I hugged them both and then the three of us ran to the correct bus. Through the rain, I showed them the bus number and made them repeat it to me as we boarded. We were soaking wet and cold, but we were safe. That was the end of a very long first day of school for all of us.

Summer Vacation

WE USED to spend two weeks during the summer at The Lido, a famous summer beach resort located south of Venice in Italy. It was a beautiful place with hot white sand and clear blue waters. My mother loved to languish in the sun, reading and relaxing.

My father was more active at the beach. He would build these huge, elaborate sand castles. People would come and admire the intricate castles complete with moats and towers, and decorated beautifully with colorful seashells. The three of us kids would help by finding seashells, bringing buckets of water to fill the moats and tugging buckets of sand to add to the creation.

My father also loved to dig deep holes in the sand and bury us. One of the funniest things my father and I did was bury the twins up to their waists – they were actually standing up in the holes my father dug. Then we would shape the sand in front of them so it looked like they were sitting down with their legs straight out in front of them, covered in sand.

The best part was waiting for an unsuspecting person or couple to walk by. My father and I would wait until we were sure they had seen the twins who looked like they serenely sitting and playing in the sand. Then we would run over yelling and shouting and jump up and down on their little fake sand-legs. The onlooker would gasp in horror at our antics while the twins screamed with laughter. The four of us would whoop it up while my mother watched, shaking her head at our performance. We loved it! The person we had tricked usually hurried by with a disgusted look on his or her face but we did not care. We would quickly smooth out the sand and create new legs and wait in anticipation for our next victim. This went on until the twins got bored or cold. Then we would let them out of their sand holes.

One day when we were vacationing at the beach, I asked my mother if I could go up to the hotel room to change and read or play a game. She nodded but told me to take the twins since it was getting close to lunchtime. I went and got my sisters and we walked across the sand to the hotel which was located right on the beach. It was a very large and tall hotel, about 10 or 11 stories high. We had to catch the elevator at the bottom of the hotel in the garage.

All hotel keys were kept at the front desk and for security reasons, it was required that if you left your room to go somewhere, keys had to be left at the front desk. So, that meant we had to get on the elevator at the ground floor, go to the first floor to get the key from the front desk and then have to wait for the elevator again to get to our floor. There was only one elevator for the whole hotel and it seemed to me that the wait for the elevator was *excruciatingly* long.

At my age, patience was not a real strength. I decided to make my sisters hold the elevator while I went and got the key. I knew it would only take a few seconds to run over and ask for the key. I also knew how to hold the elevator doors open so I figured they could too – besides there were two of them.

The problem was that this was an older elevator and did not have "Open" and "Close" buttons. When we got to the first floor, I showed the twins how to hold their hand over the beam of light between the elevator doors and how to push on the elevator door where the light was if the door began to close. Both Michelle and Diana were reluctant and afraid but I *ordered* them to obey me. I never even considered the fact that their little hands barely covered the elevator light.

I ran over to the desk and asked for the key. As soon as the attendant handed it to me, I heard the twins and my heart sank. I hurled myself around the desk just in time to see their petrified faces as the doors to the elevator slowly shut. As the elevator began to move upward I could hear their voices in uniformed terror, "*Leeeeeeeeeeee!*" I tore up the stairs and paused at each floor hoping the elevator would stop but it kept going. I could hear my sisters and the "*Eeeeeeeeeeeeeee!*" getting fainter as the elevator kept rising.

Breathless, I raced up the stairs yelling, "Everything is okay! *I'm coming!*" even though I knew they could not hear me. Finally, around the 9th floor I heard the elevator stop and the doors open. I could tell because the crying noises went from a faint, "*Leeeeeeeee*" to *LEEEEEEEEEE*!" I ran as fast as I could down the hall only to see the doors closing again! I banged on the closed doors and pressed the elevator button but I could hear the elevator now going down. Again I followed the "*Eeeeeeeeeeeee*" sound. I was taking the stairs two at a time and I was now frantic with worry and fear. Losing my sisters on an elevator was not good. Not good at all.

This time the elevator stopped on the 4th floor and I got there in time. There was an older couple in the elevator trying to calm the two little girls. Flushed and out of breath, I reached the elevator doors. Michelle and Diana were huddled in a corner, tears pouring down their cheeks, obviously completely devastated and terrified. When they saw me, they both wailed in unison and reached for me. I gathered them into my arms. We got off the elevator and I tried to dry their tears but they were still too upset and clung to me.

I finally got to our room on the 7th floor. I was shaking all over. Sure enough, a few minutes later my parents arrived. One look told them something was terribly wrong. Still wrapped in their beach towels, my sisters were sitting on the bed with me beside them, a hangdog, guilty look on my face. My mother demanded to know what happened. Both the twins started to wail again as I tried to explain. I even had the nerve to try and exonerate myself by telling my mother that the twins had failed in their duty to hold the elevator. I got the, *"Do you know how old your sisters are? They are too little to be able to do the same things you do, etc."* lecture.

From that day on, for the rest of the vacation, my sisters refused to enter the elevator. Guess who got the responsibility of walking them up and down and up and down the stairs *three* and sometimes *four* times a day? You guessed it. I learned a good lesson that vacation since I had to perform this service for over a week.

Ski Trips

WHILE STATIONED in Vienna, we went skiing every year.

Our favorite place was Schi-Schule St. Oswald. It was located just north of Villach in Kaernten Province (also known as Carinthia) in Austria. My parents took lessons from Armin – a very handsome ski instructor who was

The Small Town of St. Oswald in the Late 1960's

halfway in love with my mother. My sisters and I were enrolled in our appropriate age and skill-level classes.

When the twins were really little, they went into a daycare at the school where they were encouraged to try skiing, but they also went sledding and did other fun activities. My mother would dress them in identical, brightly colored ski suits so it was easy to spot them. They wore little tiny skis and we always got a kick out of seeing them try to use the "baby-lift." It was a rope lift that continually moved and the little kids would grab hold and the rope would drag them up a very short, gentle slope. Then they would try to "ski" down, usually ending up on their backsides, but they loved it. I was put in the class for beginning skier's ages 5 to 10. I began learning to ski at 5 years old.

As I got older, I graduated to more difficult classes until I ended up skiing with the adults. I skied with my mother and father under the tutelage of Armin. Every morning we would follow Armin around the mountain while he yelled at us to *"Bend knees! Ya! Keep skis together! Ya! Ya! Lean into curve!"* At noon we'd go to lunch and then in the afternoon, my mother and father and I would ski together.

I loved skiing with my parents but sometimes they could be so *slow*! They liked to ski down the mountain a little ways, then stop and wait for everyone to catch up, then start out again and stop. Start, stop. Start, stop. To me, this was tremendously boring. I loved to streak down the mountain in a blaze of speed, whooshing by everyone. My parents would only shake their heads and tell me to wait for them at the lift.

As my sisters got older, they were enrolled in a ski class for youngsters. Their ski instructor was Günter who had been teaching kids to ski for many years. The way he got the children to lean forward and bend their knees while on skis was to use a "Smarties tactic." (Smarties are the European equivalent of M&M's.) He'd toss the candy on the snow as he skied with the children directly behind him.

To grab at the Smarties, the kids had to bend their knees and lean forward. It was a hoot to watch him skiing so slowly with 10 or 12 little children in a line right behind him. "A mother duck and her ducklings," my mother used to say. Günter was a good teacher and incredibly patient. He taught my sisters well. They became quite good skiers.

The better I got as a skier, the more I participated in the local races they staged at the resort. I won a few silver and bronze medals of which I was very proud. So was Armin who would congratulate me loudly when he saw our family at dinner, embarrassing me terribly.

Our last trip to Schi-Schule St. Oswald was when I had just turned 10 and I had a momentous crush on a very cute ski instructor named Geoffrey. I thought he was the most handsome man I'd ever seen. (He was also 10 years older than me!) My heart would skip a beat whenever I saw him. I was still enrolled in Armin's ski class but sometimes our groups got combined.

There were a few times I remember riding the ski lift up with Geoffrey, barely able to speak I was so tongue-tied. Armin thought this was very funny and teased me mercilessly. I can still picture what Geoffrey looked like. He was tall and lean with dark hair and strong features. He was so tan that when he smiled, his white teeth blazed. Made my heart beat like I'd just run a marathon at top speed. I often think about the group of ski instructors we became close to. When we moved to Paris a few years later, we went back to the resort. Armin was still there and still the same, but that is a story to come later.

Lunchtime on the mountain was great. We'd pick my sisters up from their ski school and head for the restaurant. It was a typical ski resort restaurant – large, loud and rowdy. The smells of French fries and cooking meats assailed the senses immediately upon entering. After a morning of skiing, all of our stomachs would be growling with hunger.

After shedding numerous layers of coats, scarves, hats, gloves and thick sweaters, we'd sit with sighs of relief. The ski boots we wore were heavy and wore out the muscles in our legs. My sisters and I never varied on the meals we ordered. I always had a dark bread sandwich and a hot chocolate with *no* whipped cream. The meal was an open-faced sandwich with dark rye bread, ham and pickles. If I were at the resort right this moment, I would unhesitatingly order that same exact meal. It still makes my mouth water just thinking about it.

My sisters always ordered hotdogs and hot chocolate *with* whipped cream. The hotdogs were not the "American" version. These were fat, juicy sausages served in thick French bread with mustard. The mustard, as you can imagine, ended up more on their little faces than in their stomachs. After lunch, we'd drop the twins off again and head back up the mountain for an afternoon of skiing.

Eating Out in Europe

MY MOTHER has always been a pretty picky eater (something she would never admit). I recall that there were a few times when we went out to dinner during our stay in Austria where my mother sent her food back. It is considered by Europeans to be a very rude "American" thing to do, but that did not stop my mother.

One night we were at a very nice Austrian restaurant. My sisters and I ordered our favorite: Wiener Schnitzel. This is a delicious meal of veal, which is battered and cooked, and the best part was it also came with French fries. I think my father had a large bowl of goulash or stew. My mother ordered the duck special.

When the meals were served, we dug in while my mother looked distastefully at the duck she'd ordered. She took her fork and poked at it and then finally touched it. With a low, "*Eeek*!" she pulled her finger back and told my father that the duck was cold and raw. She *refused* to eat raw, uncooked meat. She haughtily waved the waiter over. She explained that the duck was not cooked. The waiter babbled back something in German but my mother was determined and pantomimed that she did not want it unless it was cooked. My father remained silent, watching. Finally, the waiter shrugged his shoulders, picked up the plate and took it back to the kitchen. My mother nodded her victory and gave a satisfied, "Hrrmph."

A few moments later, loud voices and crashing sounds were heard from the kitchen. This quaint restaurant was a small, intimate place and it was very obvious that someone in the back was extremely upset. My mother looked around to see what was happening. Suddenly, the doors to the kitchen burst open and out marched the chef. He was a big burly man with a tall white chef's hat perched upon his bald, sweaty head. He was holding the plate of duck in one hand and he was very angry. With his nostrils flaring, he stomped over to our table and glared at my mother.

He pointed to the duck and let out a stream of German words, each chopped at the end like he was scolding a child. My mother said not a word, just looked at him wide-eyed. My father, knowing my mother had probably not understood one word, leaned over and whispered, "He says that there is nothing wrong with this duck. It is *smoked* duck and it is supposed to be served cold. It is a specialty and a highly favored one. He has won awards for this dish."

Silently my mother quickly nodded at my father, not wanting the irate chef thinking she wasn't paying attention and turned back to receive another barrage of strange words. My mother was speechless and did not know what to do. The entire restaurant had turned silent and the clientele were watching the spectacle with big eyes. Finally, my mother found her voice and said, "Ya. Ya. Okay. Is good. I will eat it. Ya. Danke. I'm so sorry. My mistake."

My father then decided my mother had been embarrassed enough. He stepped in and began to appease the chef with words of gratitude and apology, noting that the other dishes were absolutely perfect and that my mother had just not understood the uniqueness of the "fine cuisine" that was being offered in this "high quality establishment." Somewhat mollified, the chef grunted and placed the duck dish in front of my mother with a flamboyant gesture now that he was victorious. The restaurant clientele laughed while my mother sat there, red-faced and uncomfortable. Now she had to confront the unenviable prospect of actually having to eat this cold, slimy duck just to appease the chef.

After the "episode" was over, we went back to enthus-iastically attacking our meals while my poor mother timidly picked at the grey, pickled-looking duck. She ate lots of bread. We went home satiated while my mother was probably starving. Important lesson learned, though. Never confront a German chef when he's right and you're not. You will lose every time.

The other time my mother made a fatal error in judgment happened when we were having lunch at a café in the small town of St. Oswald. She ordered a sandwich that came with a basket of French fries.

In Europe, they often serve French fries in a straw basket with a napkin on the bottom – presumably to soak up the grease. French-fries are also considered edible no matter how undercooked they are – probably because they are potatoes. My mother does not like her French fries undercooked. She decided, after looking at the basket she was served, that she would send it back and ask that the French fries be cooked appropriately.

Our server looked at her, puzzled, when she proffered the basket and said she wanted it to be cooked more. He shook his head but my mother was adamant. "I want these French fries cooked completely!" she said authoritatively. The young, thin server swirled and headed for the kitchen, basket of French fries in hand.

My father looked at my mother with raised eyebrows, a question on his face. My mother caught his look and said, "Hey, in a restaurant, the *customer* is always right. If you have been served something that is not what you wanted, you have every right to send it back and ask that it be cooked as you request." Satisfied that she had made her point, she took a big bite of her sandwich.

A few seconds later, out came the server holding a small basket high above his head. I could see smoke rising out of the top of the basket and I inwardly grimaced. *This* was not going to be pretty. With a smirk, the server placed the basket next to my mother and twirled away. My father burst out laughing when he saw what had been done to my mother's French fries. The cook – *obviously* not happy with the request to "cook the contents completely" – must have decided to place the basket, French fries and all, under the broiler. The whole mess of French fries was completely black, burnt to a crisp, including the napkin. The edges of the basket were scorched and black smoke continued to swirl upward as the fries cooled. My father, in between gusts of laughter said to my mother, "Well, honey – " he paused, "You did ask for them to be *thoroughly* cooked!" He cracked up again, which caused all of us to start giggling.

The look on my mother's face told me that my father was in dangerous territory. I think he realized it too because he quickly squelched his amusement and told us to pay attention and eat our lunches. He winked at me when he said it, so I knew he was enjoying the whole incident. Meanwhile, my mother stoically endured the hilarity and gently pushed the basket of fries to the edge of the table, hoping, I am sure, for 'out of sight, out of mind.' That was the last time I ever saw my mother send anything back in a European restaurant.

Rockville,
Maryland

1971 - 1972

Our Brief Return to the U.S.

AFTER OUR five-year stint in Austria, my father was reassigned to CIA headquarters in Langley, Virginia. For my father, this was akin to an assignment in "hell." CIA headquarters was a stuffy, bureaucratic place filled with power struggles and political turmoil. For the next year, he worked at Langley and kept his eyes and ears tuned for other assignments.

Our House in Rockville, Maryland

Meanwhile we moved into a two-story house in Rockville, Maryland – a town about 40 minutes from downtown Washington, D.C. It was a red brick house and had a tiny deck in back. The backyard was large and sloped upward. Behind the yard was a large park with a wooded, forest-like area and a small open space containing a few pieces of playground equipment.

My Uncle Bruce, Aunt Barbara and their son John came to visit us during our year in Maryland. My Uncle Bruce is a paraplegic. He injured himself in 1956 after he graduated from Harvard. He wanted to be a pilot more than anything. He was in the Air Force learning to parachute when he slipped and fell off a jump tower. The accident paralyzed him 100 percent below the waist. At the time he was engaged to his college sweetheart – Barbara.

Against great pressure from their families, Barbara and Bruce decided to carry through on their vows to marry. Barbara's family refused to host or attend the wedding, so my father's parents hosted the ceremony for them. Although the doctors told Bruce that he would not live past the age of 35, at the time of this writing, he is in his 70's.

Uncle Bruce learned how to drive even though he has no use of his lower body. He was also the first paraplegic to design, build and fly a glider plane. This amazing accomplishment put him in the Book of World Records. He is someone to be greatly admired for his ingenuity and perseverance in the face of such a disability.

During their visit to our house, Uncle Bruce brought a vehicle that he had rigged for himself. It looked like a small tank in the style of a dune buggy – almost like a miniature Humvee. With its huge wheels and enormous power, it easily crawled up our back hill, even with all four of us kids (John, my sisters and myself) and Bruce sitting in it. After getting up the hill, we left the backyard and headed for the park behind our house. It was like riding in a miniature tank. It drove over small trees, large rocks and made bushes bend back and break. We were whooping it up every time we drove over a tree or made it over a bunch of rocks. It was not speedy, but it was powerful. We begged Uncle Bruce to take us out again, but the visit was short, Bruce got tired easily, and none of us were old enough to drive. But I never forgot the power of his unique "tank/dune-buggy."

When I started the 5th grade at Rockville Elementary School, I was placed in a "special education" class because my education from K-4th grade had been overseas. The administration did not even bother to check my level of learning. I was in a class where they were teaching stuff I had learned in the 2nd and 3rd grades. I recall that I was seated next to a boy who did nothing but bounce a pencil against a piece of paper all day long. He held the pencil so just the tip would bounce up and down, leaving tiny little black dots on the paper.

By the end of the day, the boy's piece of paper was black from the pencil-leaded dots. The whole time he did this, he had a complete blank look on his face. The teacher would come over and try and get him interested in doing some kind of art or an assignment. After she was satisfied that he was going to do it, she'd leave him alone to attend to some other needy child and I would watch as he would turn the paper over or get a new sheet from his desk, and start the pencil-thing again.

I was mystified as to why he would do this. I started to copy him and found that if I concentrated on just the bouncing pencil, it was actually quite relaxing. Every once in awhile, I would take my pencil out and do the "pencil-dance." Things changed, however, when my mother discovered what was happening. She had no idea that I had been placed in a "special education" class until she asked to look at my homework. I told her I didn't have any. She was appalled and asked me what I was doing in class. I told her it was the same stuff I learned before. I also showed her the "pencil" activity and she immediately became more alarmed. She sharply told me it was a *weird* activity and it was not what I was supposed to be doing.

Angered, my mother marched over to the school and asked to see my teacher. To this day, my mother cannot understand how any teacher could just sit back and leave a child in a special education class when it was very obvious the student had an intelligence far above the level of the class. My mother demanded to see the principal. She asked why my sisters and I had not been tested or even talked to.

The principal had no satisfactory answers, but the impression he gave her was that because we had lived overseas, he believed the level of education received was far below the American standards. In fact, it was quite the opposite. The education we received overseas was far more comprehensive with much higher standards than the education provided in American schools. Very quickly my sisters and I were moved to the top classes where we were closer to our actual education levels. It was one experience my mother never forgot and she made sure to check at every school we entered after that.

The Mustard Story

THERE IS one particular episode I remember happening during this year. My mother will not appreciate that I am including this event as part of my memoirs, but I *love* to tell this story. One evening my father was going to be home late. This meant that the steak my mother had put out to defrost was going to be her responsibility. I knew she was not happy about this (I was usually pretty good about "reading" my mother's moods). She was determined, however, to make the best of it.

As she started getting the meat ready to grill, I set the kitchen table. Then, I got up on the far end of the kitchen counter and sat to watch. My mother liked to spread a thin layer of mustard around the edges of the steak to add a unique taste. It was always delicious. Steak and salad was my favorite meal so I was looking forward to dinner.

My mother got out the French's Mustard – the kind that comes in the little yellow plastic container with a twist-top. As you probably already know, to open the mustard, you have to twist the top to the right. This opens the container top enough to let the mustard through when you squeeze the container. Turning the top to the left closes the container.

My mother took the mustard, twisted the top and squeezed, holding it over the edge of the steak. Nothing came out. Frowning a little, she shook the container, aimed and squeezed again. Nothing. She frowned some more and twisted the top the other way. Aimed and squeezed. Nothing. She squeezed harder. Still nothing. My mother was now visibly frustrated. I was trying very hard not to giggle. Again she twisted and again she squeezed. Muttering out loud to herself, she squeezed harder. *Nothing*! Finally, she glared at the mustard container, exasperated, angrily twisted the top, took the container and using both hands, aimed at the steak and *squeezed* the mustard with all her might. With a huge

WHOOSHING sound, the top of the mustard container flew off and the entire contents of the mustard container exploded all over the steak, the counter, the walls, the floor and – worst of all – all over the front of my mother!

With that, I could no longer control my laughter and I fell off the counter, holding my hands over my mouth to muffle my giggles as my mother stomped around the kitchen, loudly cursing, trying to wipe up the gooey, bright yellow mustard. I knew I should start helping with the clean up but I was helpless as I lay on my bed, tears of laughter streaming down my face.

Finally, I ventured back into the kitchen. My mother had calmed down and was slowly scraping the mustard off the steak. By the time dinner was ready, the kitchen was cleaned up and my mother had changed her shirt. She did not let the steak go to waste and cooked it that night. It did taste an awful lot like French's Mustard, but it was still good. All was back to normal. But I never forgot "The Mustard Steak." It still makes me giggle today whenever I remember that night. I think about how it must have felt to be my mother at that moment – absolutely furious with an innocuous, small, yellow plastic bottle of French's Mustard. Sometimes we are all too human and forget ourselves.

The Twins: Diana & Michelle with Big Sister, Leigh -- the author

Vientiane, Laos

1972 – 1974

My Introduction to a Strange Place

MY FATHER has never fit into an "office environment." He is a true field agent. Suits and ties are not an integral part of my father's wardrobe. As I explained before, he is a "jeans and cowboy boots" kind of guy. He also loves vests with lots of pockets. The more pockets a garment has, the better (a "spy" thing).

During our year back in the United States, my father kept looking for another overseas assignment. Because my sisters and I were still young, my mother and father felt a quick move to another station was important to take sooner rather than later. At this point in time, the CIA was calling for agents to do a tour in Vietnam. The problem was, however, that they had to be "unaccompanied" – meaning no family allowed. That was not going to work for my parents. My mother and father had been separated when my father was in the Marine Corps and they weren't about to do that again.

Then, in the fall of 1971, my father learned that there was a tour in Laos considered "accompanied." Knowing nothing about the country, he rushed to learn about the place and found some people who knew the area. These good men helped my father secure this tour. Laos was known as the "hot spot" where the combined "hot war," up-country support of the Hmong[*], the Lao and other tribes fighting Vietnamese invaders was a priority in the CIA. Observing and combating the political influences of the Soviets, Chinese, Vietcong and the "Phathet Lao" (a resistance

[*] 1955 to 1975 was the Period of the Second Indochina War, or - as is more commonly known - the Vietnam War. The U.S. government recruited Hmong and Lao people to fight this war. The purpose of U.S. foreign policy toward Indochina was to defend and protect peace, freedom, democracy, and independence for Indochina, Thailand and Southeast Asia, and to protect the national security interests of the United States and the rest of the free world from the communist threat and expansion.

vas also part of the job. My father was perfect for
ıd he fit right in. We moved to Laos in August 1972.

Our time in Laos was an incredible eye-opener for all of us. I still remember the day we arrived and walked off the plane. As soon as the doors to the plane were opened, I felt this tremendous blast of heat. It was like an overwhelming blanket that took my breath away and caused my body to begin perspiring immediately. The airport was tiny, run-down and everything was covered with a layer of dust. As we were soon to learn, there are only two seasons in Laos: the dry season and the rainy season. And one thing was for sure, it was always hot, hot, *hot*.

Temperatures in Laos never got below 90. My sisters were 7 years old at the time and I was 11. As children usually do, we were able to quickly adjust to the different culture and weather. During the dry season, dust settles over the country as the rice paddies dry up and the wind blows. It is scorching hot and the land feels parched. People stay inside during the hottest hours of the day. The water buffalo wander the streets in search of water. They stay covered in mud for protection from the sun.

Year round, the Lao people carry umbrellas. Umbrellas in the dry season are for protection from the sun; during the rainy season, they provide shelter from the driving rains. The rainy season is the opposite of the dry season. It is as though the skies decide to save every drop of water possible during the dry season and then unleash the reservoir of water in torrential rains for months. It rains, rains, *rains* all the time and it is *muggy*. The air feels dense and there are huge monsoons that swoop over the land. Even if you try and protect yourself from the rain falling from above, you will still find yourself walking in flooded streets with water up to your knees.

Living in Laos exposed us to a vastly different culture. It was completely opposite to the elegance and sophistication of Europe. Although they were very poor, the Lao people were upbeat, cheerful and friendly. They believed that Americans were extremely wealthy. Compared to what they had, we *were* rich. Most of the Lao people lived in wooden and straw huts that were built on stilts in villages scattered all over. In the very poor areas, the huts were held together with mud and had only dirt floors.

Every village had a "chief" who was in charge of the village. The men worked at various jobs while the women cooked and raised the children. The women wore brightly colored sarongs and flip-flops. They donned large straw hats to protect their faces from the sun. The men also wore sarongs but usually in dark colors. Women carried large baskets on their heads as they walked to and from the market. The way they balanced these huge baskets filled with food was amazing.

At the market or in town, it was always very noisy and bustling with activity. People would be bartering loudly over produce or products. There were always children running to and fro yelling, coming up to us and trying to sell us Chicklets – the American chewing gum. Their grimy hands would hold these packets of Chicklets in front of us and they would jabber, "Chi-lets! Chi-lets! You buy? You buy?" Even if you shook your head and waved them off, they would often follow and wait for you to begin to purchase something, then surge forward, waving their packets of gum, begging you to buy some. It was overwhelming.

I also never forgot the stench of the market place. There were so many people and so many booths all stuck closely together. The market was huge and almost maze-like in its construction. It smelled of incense and leather, sweat and straw, gas fumes and dust, with a vague underlying smell of rotting fish.

Once you reached the produce and meat area, the smell was overpowering. I used to walk through this area holding my nose. I hated the smell. And the sights at the meat area would turn anyone's stomach. There were rabbits skinned and hung, ducks and chickens beheaded and lying side by side, and lots and lots of fish lying atop melting ice, their dead eyes following you around. Whenever possible, I avoided the this part of the market.

There were things I saw in Laos that made me sad. There were dogs that roamed about who were mangy and terribly thin. We were warned to keep clear of any animal that looked like it might be rabid because the disease was rampant. If you were unfortunate enough to get bitten by a rabid animal – be it a cat or dog or rabbit – you had to go to the medical clinic and get something like 12 shots in your stomach to combat the illness. That thought alone kept me horrified enough to keep my distance from any strange animal.

It seemed to me that there were always people begging for money or food wherever we went. The destitution and poverty, the barrenness of the land, and the desperation I saw in people's faces was heartrending. I also, for the first time in my life, felt guilty about how much I had compared to what the people of Laos had to live with. In the United States, we live a life of luxury.

The Shower

THE FIRST house we moved into was a large, grey building covered with thick green ivy. It rose high on stilts and had a set-up unlike I'd ever seen. The kitchen and servants quarters were completely separate from the house itself. In the morning, after getting dressed, we had to leave the big house, walk down stone steps to a paved path and then walk up more stairs to enter the kitchen, which was also on stilts. This worked out fine as long as the weather was nice. Once the rains started, however, things got a little overwhelming. After a few days of steady rain, the grounds were completely flooded. To get to the kitchen in the morning for breakfast, we literally had to walk through knee-deep water. My sisters had to be carried. My mother was not at all happy with this arrangement.

Apart from the flooding, there was another problem that manifested itself almost immediately upon our arrival. After we arrived and started moving in, I went upstairs to the bathroom to take a shower. The shower was erected in the middle of a huge bathroom. It was a stand-alone shower with a plastic curtain you pulled around for privacy. The curtain hung from a round iron rod.

To start the shower, there was a metal ring to pull from the ceiling and the water from the showerhead would rain straight down on your head. The whole shower was up on a sloped platform so that the water would not only go down the drain at your feet, but would also pour down over the platform to a larger drain in the floor a few feet away. '*A curious set-up,*' I thought, as I got ready and pulled the curtain around me.

I yanked on the metal ring and the warm water showered down, drenching me instantly. I suddenly felt something moving under my feet. I looked down and saw that out of the drain were crawling hundreds – literally *hundreds* of huge, black, shiny cockroaches. They poured out of the drain in a black mass of squirming bodies. I know I must have leapt at least three feet in the air and I can swear to you that as I flew, screaming from the bathroom, my feet never touched the floor once! I hollered for my mother as loud as I could, dancing frantically around, checking my feet to make sure no monstrous, black thing was crawling on me.

My mother came running. With a tortured look, I motioned her to the bathroom. She glanced inside, looked back at me with a frown, and went inside. *'Oh my God, my mother is so brave,'* I thought. When she came out, she was half angry, half puzzled. "Well?" she demanded, "What are you screaming about?"

I was mute with astonishment. I could not believe how calm she was. I reluctantly shuffled over to the bathroom door and peered inside. There was nothing there. No big monstrous cockroaches, no squirming, hideous bodies. Just water and a running shower. And that's when I *knew*. The whole bathroom setup was not to make sure the water went down into the big drain, it was for the cockroaches! They would be washed out of the small drain by the shower water. Then the water would carry them down to the bigger drain on the floor. Afterwards, they would crawl back up into the drainpipes until the next person to take a shower would start the horror show all over again. Aghast, I could not believe we were going to have to live in this abominable house.

I insisted to my mom we were going to have to move. She was not sure whether my over-active imagination was running on high, so we waited and ran a "test shower." Sure enough, the same thing happened. The sight was frightful to behold. Watching the huge, black, squirming bugs was enough to make the most hard-core horror fan feel faint and squeamish. After we discovered that the house was swarming with cockroaches due to the flooding and the location, there was no way we were staying in that house. We moved soon after.

Dang

DESPITE THE enormous drawbacks we discovered at the "Bug House," there was one good thing that happened during our brief stay and it turned out to be a blessing. It was here we first met and hired our maid. She ended up staying with us throughout our tour in Laos. Her name was Dang.

The day after we moved in, Dang came to our house in the pouring rain with her sister. My mother answered the door with me right behind her – I was curious to see who was visiting us so soon. My mother asked them what they wanted. They both looked so forlorn and anxious as they stood there with the rain pouring down on them. Dang spoke no English, which was why she brought her sister who could speak a few words.

When my mother found out that Dang was trying to offer her services to help the "madam," my mother told her "No thank you," and started to shut the door. For some reason, I stopped her. Dang looked so helpless and sad – my 9 year-old heart felt for her and I reached for her hand. I told my mother that there were lots of things she could do to help us. I stood holding Dang's hand and begged my mother to let her come and work for us.

Astonished at my behavior, my mother finally nodded, speechless with wonder at my adamant plea for this complete stranger. My mother told Dang to come back tomorrow and she could come to work. Dang's face broke out into the most beautiful smile I have ever seen and her gratitude was overwhelming. She gripped my hand, gave me a look of utter and complete thanks. Then she left with her sister, both babbling to each other in the strangest language I had ever heard.

I was so happy. I hugged my mother and thanked her. I ran back to my room, for some reason thrilled with the thought that Dang would be in our home. There must have been some connection or bond that had gripped me at that moment. It was as if someone had told me that we needed this woman in our lives. And it turned out to be the truth.

Although Dang was not much more than a child herself (as my mother has always said), she was able to successfully take over the cleaning, cooking and caring for the five of us without a moment's hesitation. We all loved her dearly. My father, of course, teased her mercilessly until she got confident enough to give it right back. I can recall my father ordering Dang in a deep, bellowing voice, "Dang! Go and get me a beer!" Dang would give him a sly look and tell him, "You go get yourself!" This always set my father off into a gale of laughter.

After the fiasco at the first house we were placed in, we were moved to a one-story house in another part of town. Dang accompanied us of course. We did not live in this house very long either. It was located next to a huge generator. This annoying piece of equipment made a loud, constant buzzing sound day and night. The nonstop noise began to drive my mother literally insane. My mother cannot even stand to listen to a dripping faucet so you can imagine what pressure was going on in her head.

The newness of the area, the huge cultural differences and the stress of just trying to make it in a completely unknown environment began to wear her down. The strain, coupled with the generator's constant, irritating buzzing sound, began to overwhelm my mother. Unfortunately, what also happened during this period was that my mother's mother – my grandmother – passed away, causing even more sadness and emotional stress.

Finally, the last straw was the evening we experienced a massive monsoon that swept through the area and knocked over a giant tree that toppled directly through the roof and into the middle of the living room. For my mother, that was

IT. She wanted to move and she wanted to move *NOW.* Quickly my father secured us another place to live. It turned out that this house was a wonderful place for all of us to finally settle into for the next 2 years.

Dang – at her feet is Lucky

Our "Lucky" House

Our House in Saladang

WE MOVED to a house that was painted a beautiful pale yellow with a large front porch and a huge yard. It was located in a small town called Saladang. A wall of stone surrounded the house; the gates at the entrance to the driveway were black and made of iron. Outside the gate, the road right in front of our house was paved whereas most of the roads were dirt. The paved part of the road went up a hill to one of the main roads where we used to catch our school bus in the mornings.

All the roads had deep ditches along each side. I learned they were called "Mekongs" (pronounced 'may-congs'). These trenches found along many roads were there to catch the water during the rainy season and prevent the roads from flooding. You did not want to fall into one of these trenches. During the dry season they were dried out, but during the rainy season, they filled up with thick, black mud and sometimes had leeches in them – or worse.

Huge, slow-moving water buffalo wandered the streets at random and the locals used the trenches to dispose of their droppings. It was not a good idea to keep the gate to the house open because the water buffalo would wander in and start eating our grass. This was a huge no-no with our gardener who took great pride in keeping the grass green, healthy and perfectly manicured.

Our gardener's name was Tonken (pronounced "tong-ken"). He was the gardener at this house for families who lived there before us. He was also the head of the Lao village that was just down the road from the house. My sisters were always over at the village playing with the Lao children.

Tonken – who spoke very little English – told Dang, our maid (who in turn translated to us), that we had a "lucky house." This was because underneath the house lived what we thought was a gecko. Geckos are lizards that can sometimes grow very large. They also eat all the bugs and spiders and other creepy-crawly things that wander under the house. This was why it was considered good fortune to have one living with you. A gecko can keep the insect invasion to a minimum – which (believe me) is a blessing. Insects grow to enormous sizes in Southeast Asia. It is *much* better to have as few as possible around. Some of the spiders I encountered were the size of my hand and let me tell you, they are *very* scary.

When we first moved in, I saw the gecko a few times. He wandered out from under the house and looked around, his beady little eyes darting back and forth. As soon as I made a movement, though, he scooted back under the house in a flash. At first, he was quite small. However, there must have been lots of good stuff to eat under our house because after about 6 months, he had grown to almost 5 feet long! He was huge, grey and scaly. He looked like a miniature alligator. That's when we realized the gecko was actually a giant lizard!

My mother was not happy because the "gecko" would come out on hot, sunny days, lie on the front porch and drape his huge body all across the cool tile. It was rather alarming to walk out the front door and see this massive lizard staring at you lazily. I often wondered if he ever considered humans part of the meal plan.

My mother would try and shoo him away (especially if we were expecting company). She'd stand there in her elegant pantsuit and high heels, flapping her small hand at the lizard, saying, "Shoo, now. Shoo. Go back under the house. *Shoo!*" Not surprisingly, this "shooing" tactic did not work – not even when she stamped her foot and yelled, "*SHOOO!*" as loud as she could. The lizard would merely roll its eyes and gaze up at her indifferently. Then she would call for Tonken.

Tonken had no fear of this monstrous lizard – he had no fear of any animal for that matter – and he'd grab the lizard by it's tail and drag the thing off the front porch, down the porch steps (it's head would go bump-bump-bump down the stairs) and push it under the house. By then the lizard had gotten the general idea and would slowly get to its feet and waddle off, completely unperturbed by his trip down the stairs. Tonken would usually be pretty breathless by then because that "gecko" weighed a ton! Satisfied that the front porch was free and clear of any surprises, my mother would return inside to await the guests.

Tonken, Our Gardener

Tricksy

ASIDE FROM the "lucky gecko," we had quite a selection of animals. We had a small, fluffy, pug-nosed dog named Lucky, a large male rabbit called Peter and a few other rabbits that kept having babies from Peter. We also had a selection of ducks and, for a short period of time, we had a tiny chicken named Tricksy.

We kept Tricksy in a small box in the garage and for a few days, she was the center of attention for my sisters and I. Tricksy was just a tiny, little yellow chicken that had no idea she was actually a pet. We tried to give her a bath under the garden spout once and she did not like that at all. She screeched and flapped her little wings in protest.

Unfortunately, Tricksy was not with us for long. One day my sisters and I went to go get Tricksy and could not find her anywhere. We asked Tonken whether he had seen her. Tonken got a very serious look on his face and shook his head. "Tricksy no more," he said. Then he made a forward motion with his hand and said, "Madam – *vroom-vroom!*"

I understood his meaning instantly but I could not believe it. I ran into the house and called for my mother. Breathless and hanging onto a shred of hope I asked her if it was true that she had just ran over Tricksy with her car? My mother, looking terribly guilty, silently nodded her head. I was appalled. "Mom!" I cried, "How could you do that? How could you run over our chicken? You killed our Tricksy!"

My mother replied, "Honey, I am so sorry but I did not mean to. She somehow got out of her box and I just didn't see her. I am really very, very sorry."

We mourned for Tricksy but were secretly relieved that we did not have to bury a squished little chicken body. Tonken took care of the remains for us. I believe that he thought it was the silliest thing in the world for us to have a chicken for a pet. He wanted to do what he did with all the other baby chickens – raise them, kill them, cook them and then eat them.

Super Ant

ONE DAY my sisters and I were in the kitchen when this enormous red ant walked out on the counter. We were so impressed with its size and boldness. I wondered out loud if it would be able to survive a series of experimental execution methods. My sisters clamored for a demonstration.

First, I took off my sandal and tried to squish it but it kept getting up and walking around like nothing was happening. Curious, I took a glass from the cupboard and filled it with water. Fascinated, my sisters and I watched as I scooped up the ant with a piece of paper and dropped it in the water. It just lay there for a while and then it started swimming and trying to climb out. Wow – we were suitably impressed that it was not drowning. My sisters started saying that we had found a "Super Ant."

I was more determined than ever to finish my mission to kill the "Super Ant," and I poured the ant into the sink and put the glass over it to smother it. For five whole minutes we watched in silence while the "Super Ant" nonchalantly walked around the perimeter of the glass with apparently not a care in the world.

Now I was very perturbed so I decided the next step was going to have to be very drastic. I pulled a carving knife out of a drawer while my sisters gasped. I slowly took the knife, lifted the glass and chopped that darn "Super Ant" in half!

"Ha!" I said. "Got you now!"

Visualize our utter amazement when the two halves of the ant started running in opposite directions! Not even being hacked in two could kill it! It really was a "Super Ant!"

Our Household

ONE OF the things my mother did not know (or perhaps suspected but said nothing) was that my sisters and I had a complete and utter ally in our maid, Dang. We were supposed to make our own beds and clean our own rooms *without* any assistance from Dang. My mother wanted to be sure we knew how to do all these things on our own. She did not want us to get too used to being "picked up after and spoiled."

She would give us instructions on what chores we were to complete. We would agree to do everything my mother told us to do. Then, acting like we were starting on our chores, we would wait for my mother to leave. After a few minutes Dang usually showed up carrying laundry or sheets for the beds. We'd run up to her and beg her to help us with our rooms. And, the sweetheart that she was, she would acquiesce even though my mother had instructed her not to. I am pretty sure my mother knew what we were up to, but she never said a word.

Behind our house was a separate long building where there was a washroom at one end and then some storage rooms, a small bathroom and a room which was made into a bedroom for Dang. Tonken lived in the village up the street and our cook, Hao (pronounced "Wah") had her home elsewhere and did not stay on the property like Dang.

Taking care of a house and all that goes with it was hard work. I was always amazed at how much Dang had to do all day. It was like she never rested. There was the overall cleaning, the windows, washing down the front porch, straightening rooms, picking up after us kids (although my mother scolded her not to spoil us so), and most of all, the seemingly endless laundry.

I never knew how hard it was to work in a place where there was no such thing as a washing machine or a dryer. Dang had to wash all our clothes in a big sink in the washroom, and then, before hanging them on the line outside to dry, she had to wring each article of clothing or bed sheet or bath towel through a *manually* operated wringer to get as much of the water out as possible. With five people, six including herself, this was a lot of laundry and a LOT of work! I remember sitting on a footstool in the washroom – which was a very open, airy room, watching Dang – who was often times helped by Hao, do the wash. The two of them would babble to each other while I found the repetitiveness and efficiency of the way they worked fascinating.

As you can imagine, during the hot/dry season, getting all the washed items dry was a cinch. It was during the rainy, windy and stormy season that trying to get everything dried out was tough. Then the washroom would have clothes hanging up everywhere trying to get them dry. As my mother often pointed out, though, it really was a moot point because as soon as you went outside, you were completely drenched by the rain anyway and ended up in wet clothes – so what was the difference?

There were other duties our help found themselves involved in that took my mother completely by surprise. One day after work, my mother came home and found out that my sisters had caught lice from playing with the Lao children. Now, before leaving for Laos, my mother had been given a book about being an "American Overseas," which described what to expect when living in a foreign country. The problem was that this book explained that American children "never" caught lice. Oh, *really?* My mother walked in the kitchen and saw Hao and Dang looking carefully through the twins' hair. When she realized what they were looking at, she was completely shocked! That was not what the *book* said – the *book* said American children could not get lice!

Both Hao and Dang were looking at my mother in amazement – probably thinking, '*What is wrong with Madam? Doesn't she know that it is normal to get lice if children are playing together?*' My mother, in disgust, immediately hauled the twins' off for a haircut – a *very short* haircut (my sisters both sobbed in unison about their hair). To offset the humiliation of the "scalping," my mother brought home Lucky as a consolation prize. Lucky was the cutest puppy. That mollified the twins' somewhat and I was ecstatic.

After that episode, very quickly, my mother appealed to my grandmother who was in upper state New York for help. My grandmother sent a case (24 bottles) of "lice-killer" medicine called A200. Then she had to turn around and send another case because my mother had to give the medicine to the whole village because they, too, wanted to be free of lice. The only other time lice became an issue was after we left Laos – but that is a story to come later.

Crawling

MY SISTERS and I used to play a game I made up called "Crawling." We would go into my sisters' room (it was the bigger room since the two of them were in there) and turn off all the lights. There were thick curtains over the windows, which completely blocked out the intense sunlight and kept the rooms cool. Thus, the room was completely dark and until your eyes adjusted, it was pitch-black.

The game consisted of one person who was "IT" and all the players (including the one who was "IT") were only allowed to crawl. No walking or running was allowed. You could crawl over or under the beds or even crawl up on the dresser if you could reach. It was a fast moving, breathlessly scary game – especially if you were my sisters who were only seven years old. Once the "IT" person found and tagged someone else (amidst startled screams), then the tagged person became the new "IT." The really scary part was that because of the darkness, you never really knew who was "IT" after awhile and that added to the fascination of the game.

My sisters loved this game and would beg me to play with them almost every night. Of course, my mother did not like the fact that it would get them so riled up and scared that they could not go to sleep. Then, because of my interference, she would make me tell them a bedtime story – something cheerful and soothing.

I have been a horror-fan for as long as I can remember. Perhaps it was all the nightmares I had as a small child that drew me to the intriguing world of the paranormal. I used to buy all the horror and supernatural comic books I could get my hands on. While my classmates were buying the "Superman," "Spiderman" and "Stories of Love" comic books, I was immersed in stories like "Lost Souls," "Tales of Terror," and "The Night of the Living Dead."

I was always asked to tell ghost stories at overnight parties with my friends.

Once, when I had some girlfriends over for a pajama party, I agreed to let my sisters sit with us while we held flashlights in a dark room and tried to scare each other. Boy was *that* a mistake. I told a tale I had just read in a comic book called, "The Hand." It was about this evil Hand that stalked people, trying to strangle them to death. The Hand's arm had this supernatural ability to grow so it could travel through drainpipes. It could even find its way up through a toilet to grab its next victim.

As the story continues, more and more people are killed and the Hand appears to be unstoppable. The people in the city are terrified for their lives. The tale finally ends with the Hand being destroyed by a hero-policeman who burns it to death, while it writhes and squirms in pain. When I think back, it probably was a pretty scary story. I am sure I embellished it with gory details that I have spared you here. For days afterward, my sisters were petrified and were too scared to even go to the bathroom by themselves (do you blame them?). My mother was really angry with me. I tried not to tell my sisters too many other scary stories for a while after that.

The Birthday Bike

ONE OF my favorite memories is the day it was Dang's birthday and my father told her he was going to get her a bike. A *brand new* bike. Dang had never had a brand new bike in her whole life. All she had were hand-me-downs or used items. She was overjoyed at the thought of getting a bike. I told her I wanted to go with her to help her pick it out.

The three of us – my father, Dang and I – headed over to the market in the station wagon. Dang was filled with excitement and asked my father over and over how much she could spend for the bike. My father told her there was no limit on the cost but she did not believe him. It was not until I told her she could get any, *ANY* bike she wanted in the whole place no matter how much it cost that she accepted it. That did not mean that Dang would forego bartering. Oh no. Bartering was a thrill for her. Even if we were going to the market for just one small thing, Dang haggled and debated with the merchants over everything. And she was darn good at it.

I don't think my father knew what he was in for when he gave Dang the go ahead to find the perfect bike. To her, that meant she was going to look at *every single* bike in the whole market to be sure she was getting the best. We both followed her for a while as she intently looked over each bike, tested bells and horns, pushed on seats for softness, and tested brakes and pedals. Finally, my father realized this was not going to be a quick "in-and-out" shopping spree. He left the two of us and found a shady spot and a beer.

I stayed with Dang and watched as she jabbered at the merchants, test-rode bikes, and complained about performance or scratches or the color of the paint. Most importantly, she bartered incessantly on the price. Finally, after a *very* long morning, she settled on the perfect bike. It was bright blue with a very soft black seat and – best of all –

it had a basket on the front and a big bell. I ran back to get my father (he was the one with the money). Dang proudly showed him her prize and explained the price – which she had bartered down to a surprising great deal. He doled out the money and Dang, with her head high, rode the bike through the marketplace like a queen, smiling broadly at everyone.

When we reached the car, my father opened up the back to put the bike in but Dang was having nothing to do with that. She told us she was going to ride her bike all the way home, showing it off to everyone around her, of course. We followed her in the car and drove very, very slowly with Dang riding ahead, proud and extremely happy.

When we finally got home, *everyone* had to come out and admire the new bike. We all gave it a test ride and praised her choice. Dang had always been fond of my father but now he was "Number One." To the Lao, "Number One" means the best. If you are "Number Ten," that is really bad. Later my father told me that if he'd known how excited and happy she was about getting a bike, he would have done it a long time ago.

Dang's Accident

AFTER WE'D been in Laos about 1-½ years, our beloved Dang had a bad accident. She had gone out on her night off and was riding on the back of a motorcycle with her boyfriend when she fell off. She sustained a very bad break to her right arm. The problem was that she did not tell anyone and demanded that her friend keep quiet. She tried to wrap the arm herself and covered it by wearing long-sleeved shirts.

I am not sure just how long she hid her injury, but I do remember that she started to get sick and would not let anyone come into her room. Because I was so close to Dang, she finally showed me the wrapping that was covered in dried blood. I ran to tell my mother even though Dang was crying and begging me not to. My mother, who'd been unaware that there was a real problem, finally ordered Dang to come out and show her the injury.

My mother slowly unwrapped the dirty bandages from the poorly covered arm. The break was very, very bad. The arm bone had actually broken completely in half and was sticking out through the skin. It was bright red, had a terrible odor and was obviously infected. Dang was crying, holding her arm and pleading with my mother not to take her to the hospital. Dang was terrified of going to the hospital. Like many other Lao people, she believed that going to the hospital meant death.

My mother, appalled at the extent of the injury was very concerned that Dang might now lose her arm. She told Dang that she must see a doctor at the hospital. She tried to assure Dang that she was not going to die. My mother told her she would take her to the doctor and that she must go and go *now*. Not sure what she would encounter at the Lao hospital, my mother refused to let me come with them. I still remember that my mother practically had to drag Dang to the car. Dang was crying and babbling, "No hospital. No hospital. Please Madam, *please. No hospital!"*

The injury to her arm was so bad she was immediately admitted and had to have an operation. They also made her stay for a recovery period because of the extent of the infection. That first day, my mother remained with Dang until she had to leave. Even then Dang begged her not to go. It just about broke my mother's heart to have to leave Dang there by herself.

Understandably concerned after seeing the horrific conditions at the hospital, my mother went to see Dang every day until she could come home. My mother would not let the twins or I visit her because she did not want us to see the dreadful and ghastly state that the hospital was in. It was poorly staffed, unsanitary and many who were there were slowly, painfully dying. The sight of it was almost more than my mother could bear and she refused to let us be exposed. I think she did the right thing.

When Dang finally came home after a few weeks, the scar on her arm was long and covered her whole forearm. It ran from her wrist to her elbow. It still red and angry-looking but the infection was gone. Dang was so happy to be home that she did not care about the scar. She had been convinced she was going to die and that she would never see any of us again so the scar was nothing. Later, though, when she went out she was always careful to cover it. Vanity exists in every society.

The Spaghetti Dinner

THE FIRST time Dang took time off to go and visit a sick relative, she brought her friend, Nang, to our home to take over her responsibilities while she was gone. My mother had told Dang that doing so was not necessary, but it was unthinkable to any of our servants that we actually do any work ourselves. My mother was finally beaten down by Dang's insistence and Nang came to stay.

Everything was going along just fine until one evening when my parents went out for dinner. My mother told Nang, whose English was very, *very* limited, that the children were to be fed a spaghetti dinner. My mother showed Nang the box of noodles, the package of beef and the jar of spaghetti and explained the basics of what to do. Lastly, she told Nang that we were not to leave the table until the three of us had cleaned our plates.

The Lao take their jobs and responsibilities very seriously and take great pride in doing a good job. That meant following orders without question. Unfortunately for Michelle, Diana and myself, we were about to experience first-hand what that meant.

When Nang called us to dinner that night, we raced inside to eat. We were starving as most kids are after an afternoon of playing. I stopped cold, though, when I saw our plates. Each plate was piled high with an extremely large portion of spaghetti noodles covered in sauce. One plate would have been enough to feed all three of us. Nang had done just what my mother told her to do. She had made the *entire* box of spaghetti noodles and cooked the whole package of beef (probably around 5 lbs) and used the whole (industrial-size) jar of sauce.

The heavily laden plates of food were only the beginning of the nightmare. After we had eaten as much of the spaghetti as we possibly could, I got up to leave. Nang had been sitting on a stool near the table watching us intently. As soon as I stood up, she said something sharply to me in Lao and pushed me back down in my chair. She was obviously upset. "Eat, eat," she urged us, gesturing with her hands toward our plates. "You *eat!*"

Both my sisters had their faces covered with spaghetti sauce were obviously very full. I saw their confusion so I tried to explain to Nang that it was too much. "Too much food," I said. "We can't eat all this. It's too much."

Nang was visibly agitated and kept pushing me back into my seat. "Eat!" she screeched at us. "Madam say eat. You *eat!*" The twins began to cry. Big crocodile-size tears oozed their way down through the sauce on their cheeks and chins. I knew if I tried to get either one of them to eat any more to appease Nang, they would both get sick. I could feel my own stomach beginning to churn.

Again and again I appealed to Nang to let us leave the table. I tried to explain that we were full. I even showed her my own stomach that was so full it was round and hard. I pushed my plate away and moved the twin's plates away from them and waved my hands, "No more, Nang. No more. Too full. No more. We'll get sick." I argued. I cajoled. I begged. But Nang would not budge. She would not allow us to leave the table. Every time I tried, she began to scream and yell at me.

I had no idea at the time that Nang was deathly afraid that if she did not enforce my mother's "order," she would be punished. The Laotian concept of Americans was so warped that she believed we actually ate like this all the time – that by some magical ability, even small children could eat endless amounts of food. It was the same way they seemed to think about money. It was like they thought we were so rich, money just flew out of our pockets whenever we wanted.

The evening seemed everlasting to us. Finally the twins gave up and just sat in their seats, staring at me hopelessly. I, too, gave up and sat silent. And so we waited. I have no idea how long we waited. Fortunately for us, my father came back to the house for something and saw us still sitting at the kitchen table. There was cold, jelled spaghetti all over the table and plenty still on our plates. As soon as Michelle and Diana saw our father, they began to wail and my father looked at me with questioning eyes. I shrugged and told him that Nang said we could not leave the table until we were done.

Nang, obviously very upset and fearful, began talking very fast in Lao about what "Madam" had said. Calming her down, my father told Nang that everything was just fine and he would deal with "Madam." He told us we could leave the table. Grateful, the three of us ran to freedom. As my father looked around, he realized that Nang had, indeed, followed my mother's orders and made dinner using all the food instead of measuring out a "normal" amount for three children.

Nang was still very upset and scared that she had done something wrong. My father had to reassure her over and over that no harm was done. After the infamous "spaghetti incident," my mother was always very careful about how she gave "orders" to the help. I also remember that we did not have spaghetti at our house for a very long time after that.

The Guard

WHILE STATIONED in Laos, we always had a guard at the house. They were Laotian guards that the embassy would hire to guard Americans who were housed off the American base. The guards usually came at dusk and watched the house and grounds at night. Most of them were nice; very few spoke more than a few words of English. Sometimes we'd have the same guard for a few weeks, but the embassy would rotate them so after awhile we'd end up with someone different.

I remember one guard in particular because I felt an instant dislike when I met him. I've often been told I have a sixth sense about people. I have been seldom wrong when it comes to feeling wary when I sense there is something not right. This guard was a rather large man and had cold dark eyes. I knew he did not like me. He probably did not like any of the "rich Americans" he was working for. I avoided him whenever possible.

Once I caught him kicking our dog, Lucky, and I yelled at him to leave her alone. He eyed me, shrugged and walked away like it was no big deal. I told my mother but she did not want to be bothered with such petty stuff and told me to forget about it. I watched that guard all the time after that and he knew it.

One day around dusk, I was getting ready to go inside after playing in the garden. The guard had been watching me, waiting, and he beckoned me to come over. He was holding something in his right hand and had it covered with his left. He smiled at me and nodded as I slowly, warily approached. I was curious. As soon as he was satisfied that I was close enough, he quickly uncovered his hand. He was holding an enormous bug. It was like a giant cockroach but it was green and it had wings. To this day I have no idea what it was. But I do know it was big and it was alive.

Still smiling, the guard lifted the bug off of his hand and in one swift movement, brought it to his lips – the thing was squirming and trying to get away – and took a big bite out of it. I still remember the shock and the hideous sound of the loud *crunching* sound it made while he bit it in half. I was so repulsed and stunned I could not move for a moment. Then he grinned at me and kept chewing. I finally found my voice and let out a blood-curdling scream. I turned and ran, completely horrified and revolted. I almost knocked my mother over as I bolted through the front door. She grabbed me and shouted at me to stop screaming. I tried to tell her what the guard had done, but I could only cry and shake.

The picture of that moment has never left me nor has the ghastly memory faded. I can even still smell the cool night air and see his face clearly. When my mother finally calmed me down enough to get the story, she was absolutely furious and ordered the guard off the premises. She reported his outrageous behavior to the embassy department. I have no idea what happened to him, if anything did, but I was glad not to ever encounter his face again.

My Horse Pywaket

I WAS given the privilege of having my own horse. My mother went with me to find the perfect horse (pony) for me. We found an American family that was leaving the country who had a horse for sale. His name was Pywaket (pronounced Pie-wa-ket). He was a short but sturdy pony with soft brown fur and a dark brown mane. The girl who owned him told me he was a great horse but warned me to be careful because he could be feisty and needed constant discipline.

I loved Pywaket on sight and my mother agreed to let me get him. We had Tonken build a barn for him. He chose a spot that was next to the wall by our house. There was a large tree in our garden next to the wall that was quite tall. Part of the tree grew over the wall and shaded a large portion of the rice paddy that was there. Tonken built a simple wooden barn-like structure that was very open and airy – essential due to the heat in this part of the world. The beauty of the whole setup was that instead of having to walk down the driveway, through the gates and around the wall to get to Pywaket, I merely climbed the tree, crawled over the wall and jumped down into the wooden pen.

Pywaket nibbling grass outside his "pen"

When we first got Pywaket and set him up in his stable, we discovered that the village children were at first scared of him but soon got curious about the large animal. Unfortunately, their inquisitiveness quickly turned to teasing, most of which was vicious and cruel. To his credit, Tonken tried to control the children but when he was away and I was at school, the children would run down to the stable. They would poke branches and throw rocks at Pywaket through the stable openings, causing my horse to become very upset. My mother also worried because this could cause an animal to become mean and turn on everyone, even those who were good to him. I was upset, too, because there were many days when I came home from school and found rocks and sticks all over the stable floor.

One day when the children came down to torment Pywaket, one of the older boys got too close. Anyone who has been around horses knows that although they give the appearance of being docile and slow moving, a horse can be lightening fast when it wants to be. This boy had a stick and was yelling and poking it at Pywaket. He got closer and closer, putting on a show of bravery for the other children. Suddenly, Pywaket snaked his head forward as fast as a whip and bit deeply into the boy's chest.

A horse bite is extremely painful. Even a nip can cause bruising. Most horses do not bite to maim unless they are scared or threatened. This boy just went too far that day and he paid for his misbehavior and cruelty. The bite left two deep holes in the boy's chest. Pywaket had bitten through the skin and some of the boy's chest had been torn away. The children fled, screaming. The injured boy ran back to the village calling for his mother. Blood was pouring from his chest and he was gasping for air. It was a very bad wound and the boy had to be taken to the local hospital.

When I got home from school, I found all this out from my mother who told me that Tonken was at the village telling the people that they had no right to demand that the horse be put to death. The Lao people believe that if an animal is dangerous, it should be killed. I knew some of the superstitions of the Lao because all the cats I ever saw, the tips of their tails were always broken. The Lao people did this when kittens were born because it was believed that this had to be done in order to keep an animal from entering the same Nirvana (heaven) as humans. Since cats were considered the animal closest to perfection, they disfigured it to make it imperfect.

Knowing the Lao ways and the fact that my horse was responsible for injuring a child, I was horrified that they might come and kill him. We found out later that Tonken had taken care of the problem and nothing would happen to Pywaket. The boy was going to be fine although he would have a deep scar on his chest. The tormenting and teasing came to an abrupt stop. When word got out about what happened to the boy, all the children avoided the stable. That made me much happier.

When things calmed down after the bite-episode, I concentrated my efforts on learning how to ride. Pywaket was a feisty, stubborn animal and it was a challenge for me to handle him. I started out riding with a light "blanket" saddle. I would like to tell you that I was able to master this spirited animal right away, but it took several months before I actually felt that I was in control. Riding every day after school became part of my daily routine.

In the mornings, as my sisters and I trudged up the road to the top of the hill where the school bus picked us up, I would see Tonken get Pywaket to take him to a nearby field where he could eat the grass and romp around. After school, I would come running down the road yelling Pywaket's name. When he saw me, he would return my greeting with a loud whinny. I knew he was glad to see me. I would quickly put my school stuff away and race to the tree, climb over the wall and jump into the barn where I would give Pywaket a big hug. Even though he'd had time to expend some energy in the field, by afternoon he was raring to go. I would put the saddle on (after about 2 months I no longer rode with a saddle, preferring to ride bare-back instead), bridle him up and away we would go.

Riding gave me an incredible sense of freedom. I rode all around the area we lived. Rice paddies and fields separated the different villages. During the dry season, the roads were hot and dusty. When the rainy season arrived, the roads turned into huge muddy lanes. There were also a few neighborhoods like ours with large houses and gated yards. In the beginning I stayed close to home but eventually my curiosity got the better of me and I ventured further and further away. Sometimes I rode for an hour –sometimes for half a day (on weekends). Every day was a new day for Pywaket and me.

One afternoon we were out, trotting along and everything was going along splendidly. Since I'd only been riding for a short while, I was still riding with the blanket saddle. It was a beautiful clear day – *hot* – and it wasn't raining which was fine with me. Riding in the rain with a soaking wet blanket saddle is really uncomfortable. We were on a dirt road passing a rice paddy when out of the blue, for no reason that I could see, Pywaket moved sideways with a jerk. Horses have this remarkable ability to move sideways without missing a beat and this can completely unseat a rider without warning. I was feeling quite proud of my riding ability so perhaps Pywaket sensed my relaxed state and decided to try and topple me for the fun of it.

At any rate, there I was in mid-air and headed for the dirt road while my horse was calmly beginning to walk away across the rice paddy. Unfortunately, my left foot got caught in the saddle stirrup as I descended. I landed with a heavy, "*OOOOF,*" and discovered that I was now being dragged along behind Pywaket as he slowly picked his way across the rice paddy!

I yelled at Pywaket to "*Stop!*" This only caused his ears to flatten and he picked up speed. Rice paddies are like plowed fields with peaks and valleys in the dirt. Because it had recently rained, the rice paddy was very muddy in the valley parts. So, there I was being dragged along, trying desperately to get my foot out of the stirrup. My back and head were bouncing up and down as Pywaket continued to walk forward, acting like it was nothing to be hauling this bouncing, gasping, muddy human around. My hair was covered in mud and dirt and I could feel my back getting scratched.

"Pywaket! Stop right now!" I yelled again which I regretted immediately as he then began to trot. My head was being pounded into the ground. I concentrated on keeping my head up and kept trying to twist my foot out of the stirrup. Desperate, I tried another approach. I began to talk sweetly, infusing my voice with false warmth. I said as nicely as I could over and over, "Pywaket, you can stop now. Stop. Time to stop." I gritted my teeth and again said in a sweet singsong voice, "Time to stop now. Oh Pywaket, you big stupid lug of a horse, *puleeeeeease* stop." For a moment, he paused and lowered his head to eat some grass. I tried to quickly lift myself up and move my foot, but that only started him moving again.

Finally, I just let myself be pulled around until he decided to halt at a particularly enticing grassy spot. As slowly and quietly as I could, I pushed my leg forward and then slipped it out of the stirrup. I was so happy to be able to stand again. I had tears of joy (and pain) flowing down my cheeks. I grabbed the bridle and fixed the saddle, which had rolled off his back and was clinging to his side. At that moment, I decided I would not ride with a saddle again. It was time for me to learn how to ride bareback. The ride home was thankfully uneventful but I had a scratched and bruised backside for about a week.

After I'd been riding for about 3 months or so, I found a road I had never ridden down before. As soon as I turned onto this road, it was obvious that Pywaket recognized where we were and he picked up speed. I enjoyed his sudden perkiness until I tried to slow him down. He ignored me and went faster. From a quick trot we went into a canter and then into a full gallop while I tried to stop him with all my might. I pulled on the reins until I was red in the face from the effort. I yelled at him to stop. It made no difference to Pywaket – he knew where we were going and by golly he was going to get there.

After a few moments at a breath-taking gallop – I was bouncing all over and had absolutely no control – Pywaket suddenly and abruptly turned to the left and headed to what I now saw was a small pond. With the amazing ability that horses have, he came to a full stop right at the edge of the pond.

From a full gallop to a complete stop meant only one thing for me: I went head-over-heels right smack into the pond. I landed spread-eagle on my back in the water with a gigantic *SPLASH!* Gasping, I sat up, drenched with smelly pond water, and watched as my now docile horse slowly walked into the pond with a look of utter joy on his face. He lay down and rolled in the cool water. I sighed. At least now I understood Pywaket's frantic pace – I am sure the promise of a romp in some cool, muddy water was irresistible.

The ride home after the pond-rolling episode was most uncomfortable for me as I was riding bareback and Pywaket and I were both covered with mud and moss from the bottom of the pond. I tried to clean him off as best I could, but it was virtually impossible to get everything off. Needless to say, the next time we went to the pond, I took a towel with me to dry him off and brush off the mud. After my initial introduction to "The Pond," I let Pywaket come back more often – especially when it was relentlessly hot. Sometimes I wanted to get in with him, but the pond was too smelly and slimy for me.

Every once in awhile, I would ride Pywaket over to some friends of ours who lived a few miles away. There were no paved roads so we usually arrived dusty, hot and thirsty. Jim Anders and his wife always welcomed us in (Pywaket got tied up in the garden surrounded by endless amounts of tasty, green grass). I would sit on the porch and cool off, gulping down delicious, ice-cold lemonade and talk to the Anders.

Sometimes I would stay and enjoy lunch or a snack before making my way home. One day, however, I found lots of reasons to stay a bit longer – six reasons to be exact. The Anders' cat had given birth to a litter of six kittens and they were about 4 weeks old. They were so incredibly cute. I had to pick each one up to feel the soft fur and watch their eyes peer curiously into mine. I really wanted to take one home but I knew with the medley of animals we already had, my mother would no allow it. I decided that while we were there, I would take one of the kittens over to Pywaket so he could see one – he was my friend after all.

Unfortunately, I did not take into consideration that maybe Pywaket did not want to be bothered with meeting a strange, mewing thing. So, not even thinking about what might occur, I walked toward him holding out the kitten and started to say, "Hey, Pywaket. Look! It's a –"

Suddenly, – *POW!* – my introduction was interrupted as I flew backwards through the air and landed about 6 feet away from Pywaket. I sat there, completely dazed and shocked while Pywaket looked at me, snorted, shook his head and went back to calmly eating. I had no idea what had just happened. Fortunately, I still held the small kitten in both hands so no harm was done there. When I looked down at the front of my shirt, I gasped. There, clearly visible, was a perfectly shaped, muddy hoof-print! Then I realized what had happened – Pywaket had kicked me! I quickly felt around my stomach area but there was no pain anywhere.

Then I understood. Pywaket wasn't trying to hurt me; he was just sending a clear message that he wanted nothing to do with the kitten. The kick had probably been more like a "kick-boxing" move where he just used his powerful leg to lift and throw rather than try to hurt or maim. I cradled the kitten as I walked back and decided then and there that I would be more wary of introducing Pywaket to other living animals. I guess the saying "live and learn" means sometimes learning the hard way.

When it came to feeding Pywaket, there was one thing that used to drive my mother crazy. Tonken spoke very little English so a decent two-way conversation was difficult at best. To this day my mother says she thinks Tonken knew and understood a lot more than he ever let on. One of his responsibilities was to make sure there was enough horse feed. We had a huge barrel of rice and oats mixed together which was kept in the garage.

From time to time, Tonken would go to my mother and tell her that he needed to get more food. She would tell him she would give him money in a day or two but he would shake his head and say he needed it now. "Right now?" my mother would ask and Tonken would nod his head affirmatively. So she would go and check the barrel. Sure enough, it would be completely empty. *'Oooooo!'* my mother would get incensed.

She would bring Tonken over, show him the barrel and explain to him very carefully that she wanted him to ask for money *before* the barrel was empty. She would point to the barrel and indicate that when there was about a quarter of food in the barrel, he should tell her. Tonken would nod his head over and over and say, "Yes, Madam, yes." The reason for this was because my mother had to ask my father to make a special trip to the Embassy in order to exchange American dollars for Lao "Kip" which was the local currency. This took time. My mother, frustrated with Tonken, used to say, "What? Does he think I have a tree somewhere that grows money?"

Inevitably, weeks would pass and Tonken would appear before my mother, telling her he needed money for food. The same demand for money *"right now"* would occur. My mother would check and the barrel would be totally empty again. It confounded her. I think she secretly believed he did it on purpose just to see her get frustrated and annoyed.

A Close Call

IN LAOS, all food and drink had to either be put into an airtight, sealed container or placed in the refrigerator. No matter how clean you kept the house or kitchen, the roaches and other insects were just too many to try and eliminate. Therefore the refrigerator was where you put any open container – even if you were just leaving the kitchen for a moment. In fact, every six months we were required to give urine and stool samples to the medical clinic (as well as have our shots – *ugh*).

My mother would give us the containers for the samples and after we had done our duty, she would put them all in the refrigerator (correctly labeled, of course) to preserve until she could take them to the clinic the next day. We thought this was a riot. I would send my sisters off into gales of laughter by acting like I was a cook. I would put on a whole show of opening the refrigerator and finding one of the containers and acting like I thought it was some kind of exotic chocolate. My mother was *not* amused.

I was required to clean and brush Pywaket every day because the horse flies could be terrible. His hooves also had to be carefully looked after and cleaned – especially during the rainy season because dampness could cause infection. I cleaned his hooves with bleach on a daily basis. My mother would buy the industrial-size bleach container since I used so much. Instead of lugging this huge container back and forth from the house to the barn, I would fill a regular drinking cup with the amount of bleach I needed.

One late afternoon, my parents were gone and I was getting ready to clean and brush my horse. I got out a cup and filled it with bleach. I suddenly remembered something else I needed to get and I automatically – without even thinking – put the cup in the refrigerator while I ran off. Remember, *all* open containers went into the refrigerator. The next thing I knew, I heard one of the twins screaming and screaming. Alarmed, I rushed back to the kitchen where I saw Diana on her knees screaming at Michelle. With one glance I realized that Michelle had opened the refrigerator, thought the cup of bleach was lemonade and took a big gulp. Michelle was gasping and writhing on the ground, holding her throat and she was turning blue.

I quickly pulled Diana back, yelled at her to be quiet and ran to the cupboard under the sink where the bleach container was. I scanned the warning label and read that, "if swallowed induce vomiting by giving the victim milk to drink." I whirled and grabbed the milk from the refrigerator. I dragged my sister by the arm through the kitchen, past the dining room to the bathroom and there forced a half-gallon of milk down her throat.

Even in my alarmed state, I was surprisingly calm. I also knew that it would not please my mother if Michelle vomited all over the kitchen floor (another of the many unspoken rules drilled into me by my mother – vomiting was not allowed to be done *anywhere* except in the bathroom). Thank goodness, just as the bleach label had said, Michelle started vomiting and coughing up the milk and the bleach. The smell was awful. Diana sat next to her sister, tears streaming down her face. She was afraid her sister was dying. I was also terribly anxious about what might happen.

As soon as I saw Michelle was breathing, I ran to the phone right outside the bathroom on the small desk and dialed the medial clinic. My parents had wisely posted all important phone numbers on the wall. I blurted out the story to the receptionist who quickly got a doctor on the phone.

I told him my parents were not home and that I was the only one there. He told me he wanted me to check Michelle's "vitals." I put down the phone (no cell phones or portable phones back then), went and grabbed Michelle again and dragged her to the desk. She was still coughing but her face was no longer blue and she just looked like she felt very ill. The doctor slowly asked me questions and had me check her skin, breathing and eyes. He felt confident that most of the bleach had probably been vomited up but still thought she should get checked. He asked me if I knew where my parents were. I told him they were about 2 miles down the road at a friend's house. The doctor told me to call them and have them take Michelle to the clinic.

I did as the doctor told me. As soon as I called, my parents rushed home. By that time, Michelle was sitting up and I had helped her put on a fresh shirt and shorts. Most of the damage was in the bathroom and my mother told me that she would get Dang to clean it up. My mother took Michelle to the clinic where she was found to be just fine. There was no permanent injury (thank goodness). The doctor who saw Michelle was the one I talked to on the phone. He asked my parents to call him when everyone was home.

When my parents called the doctor, he asked to speak to me and told me he thought I was the bravest and most courageous eleven-year old girl he'd ever known. He said I had done all the right things and saved my sister's life. He made me feel very good. My parents praised me as well, although I did get a lecture about never leaving an open container of bleach around anywhere – ever! I had such a mix of emotions – I felt bad about the bleach and that it was my fault Michelle drank it – but then I also felt like a hero for saving my sister's life. How ironic is that?

Touched by Death

I CONSIDERED Pywaket my best friend. I confided in him about everything. I believe he could tell when I was upset about something. If I got in trouble or was sad, I would go out to the stable and talk to Pywaket, pouring my heart out, and he would gently nuzzle my hand.

After I stopped riding with the blanket saddle, I learned quickly how to ride bareback. It takes much more muscle and coordination to stay on a horse bareback. I would grip his mane tightly (thank goodness it did not hurt him) and squeeze my legs around his wide middle. When we galloped, I hung on for dear life, loving the absolute sheer exhilaration of his speed and strength.

As time went on, I was able to experiment with different things. I even got to the point where I could stand up on Pywaket's back and stay on while he walked. I felt like a circus performer. I taught him to trust me enough to where I could pat him on the rump – signaling I was about to do a trick – step back and jump up onto his back. I'd balance for a second and then stand with my arms stretched out in a victory stance. I was very proud of my ability to gain Pywaket's trust as well as my own gymnastic ability.

My friend Millie lived about 20 minutes away from me. She had a horse named Flicka (yes – just like the book) and we often rode together. She was not as diligent at exercising her horse daily as I was. This was probably because she did not have *my* mother as her mother. Every once in awhile I would ride over and persuade her to come out with me. She lived in a big house with tons of windows, but it was always dark inside because her mother kept all the curtains shut. Her parents did not exactly encourage "company."

One day I rode over and looked for Millie. I could not find her anywhere so I knocked on the front door. Millie's mother answered. She looked terrible. She told me to go away – that Millie was not going to be able to play today. I asked her why but she just shook her head and shut the door in my face. She looked as though she'd been crying. I stood there for a moment not knowing what to do.

I turned to go back to Pywaket who was standing quietly, munching on some grass, when I saw Millie's gardener waving at me to come over. He knew I was Millie's friend and that we always went riding together. He told me that Flicka had gotten very sick and had an accident. He told me it was colic – or at least that's what I figured out from his broken English.

Apparently, Flicka, who was very weak from the illness, had left the stall to drink some water out of the large fountain they had in the back yard. She made it to the fountain but then her knees must have buckled and she fell partway into the fountain and drowned. I was sickened and devastated by the news. I was also sure Millie was suffering badly. What a horrible way for a beautiful animal to die.

My friend was never the same after that. I, too, was changed. I worried incessantly about the health of Pywaket. I could not bear the thought that he might get sick. He never did, but death had touched me in a way I had never felt before.

The American School of Vientiane

THE AMERICAN school was located on the KM-6 base. This American base contained about 100 small "bungalows" that housed mostly USAID "aid" families as well as some Air America families. In addition to the housing, there was also the school and a major electric power station. A stone wall and fencing surrounded the base, which supposedly designated it a "secured facility." My father tells me it was probably easier to break into the base than into our own house. There was a guard station at the base entrance and a guard was supposed to be on alert at all times. I only remember the guards as either sleeping or looking like they needed a good night's rest.

I attended the American school for 6th and 7th grades. My 6th grade teacher was a grandmotherly-type whose name was Mrs. Diffley. I have never forgotten her. She is one of the few teachers I can still remember from middle school. She knew just how to handle a classroom full of rowdy, energetic and hormone-producing kids. In my case, especially, she was exceptionally caring in how she treated my abundance of endless energy. My mother was very grateful.

During one of the first days of school, there was a group of parents, including my mother, who came to the school. As they observed my class frolicking around the playground during recess, one of the mothers asked my mother if I was on Ritalin. My mother was shocked and told the woman of course not. The woman proceeded to explain that it looked like I was a child out of control and probably needed medication.

My mother – rightfully in a huff – told the woman that I was a perfectly normal child with lots of energy. My mother spoke to Mrs. Diffley about it. Mrs. Diffley was also in agreement that I certainly did not require medication. "Just good, solid love and a pat on the back when they do something right," Mrs. Diffley used to say.

I quickly adapted to the new school. Every day, once the recess bell rang, I was always one of the first to race back to the classroom. Mrs. Diffley would wait for me outside the classroom door and greet me with her hands outstretched saying, "Leigh, recess is over. You are not supposed to run in the halls. How many times do I have to tell you? It's now time to calm down and *relax*. Calm down, now, and *relax*. I want you to go straight to the blackboard and erase everything on it for me and then <u>sit down</u>."

Cleverly, by giving me something to do once inside the classroom, she allowed me some time to catch my breath and control my energy. Then I could sit down and pay attention. There was only one time when I knew I had ruffled her serenity and composure. It was a particularly sweltering day and most of the playground equipment was too hot to play on. We ended up sitting in the shade instead of running around.

As soon as recess was over, I was up and running down the school hall to my classroom. All around our school there were tons of water-bottle dispensers. We were not allowed to drink any water out of the faucets because it might be contaminated, so any water we drank had to come from bottled water. (At home our cook would boil large amounts of water to purify it and keep the purified water in a container in the refrigerator.) In those days, the water bottles were made out of glass rather than plastic.

Well, there I was, running pell-mell down the hall, doing a zig-zag-type of darting one way then the other (no reason why – just felt like doing it) when I heard Mrs. Diffley yelling at me. I was so shocked because she *never* yelled at me. I started to lift my head to see her and ran straight into a water dispenser, knocking the glass water bottle over with a supreme – *CRASH* – of glass and water. The noise was deafening and my heart stopped in fear and panic. Then I saw Mrs. Diffley running. I mean she was actually moving like an Olympiad down the hall yelling at me to, *"Get back!"*

I reeled back and landed on my butt, feet kicking frantically backward, pushing and wiggling myself away from the massive damage spreading across the hall floor. I was scared to death. With amazing grace and speed – in her shin-length brown conservative dress and old-lady black shoes – Mrs. Diffley leapt like a deer over the glass and water and swooped me up in her arms, pulling me back even further from the dangerous shattered glass.

By now other kids had started coming down the hall but teachers were appearing from everywhere, waving them back. There I was, the guilty party, gripped by a pair of lethally strong arms, tears pouring down my face and my heart beating madly. After the damage assessment was done and the janitor crew was called, Mrs. Diffley wiped away the tears and whispered, "My dear child. Now you need to relax and be calm. And *no running* in the halls, young lady! How many times do I have to tell you?" She was my savior. Naturally she had to tell my mother – to my dismay. Like my mother needed reminders about what happens when you raise a child who started running before she could even walk.

Show and Tell

WHEN MY sisters were in the 3rd grade, they had a daily "show and tell" time where a student would get up in front of the class and share some tidbit of information. Usually most children brought up stories about their pets or where they went on vacation or some equally innocuous subject. My sister, Diana, however, had something to share with the class that turned out to be very, very different.

Diana did not want to participate in "show and tell" and told the teacher so. Despite her protestations, the teacher insisted that she contribute along with everyone else. So, when it was Diana's turn to "show and tell," she reluctantly stood up and walked to the head of the classroom. She turned, frowned, stuck out her lower jaw (a sure sign of her displeasure) and told her peers that she did not really have anything to "show" because she was not able to bring her father to class but she did want to "tell" what recently happened to him.

Looking very serious, Diana told the class that her father had been *"shot in the head, the arms and the legs and was in the hospital."* While her classmates were instantly riveted, the teacher was appalled. She asked Diana if it was really true to which Diana convincingly told her that, "Yes, it really happened. My Daddy is in the hospital and he's all bloody." Still reeling from the awful information, the teacher quickly told Diana to sit back down.

At her next opportunity, the teacher called my mother and asked, "Mrs. Platt – I am so sorry to hear what has happened. Is Mr. Platt alright?"

My mother, understandably very puzzled said, "Well, yes. He's just fine."

"Oh good," said the teacher. "I hope you are doing well, too."

"Uhhh, well, yes – thank you – I am fine."

After hanging up the phone, my mother felt very confused but decided that the teacher was probably married to someone who worked with my father and knew about something that my father would later share with her. It was not until the phone began ringing off the hook with concerned friends and parents of children from Diana's class that my mother realized something was very wrong. Immediately she called my father and the conversation went something like this:

My mother: "Hi honey. It's me."

My father: "Hey there darling. How is everything?"

My mother: "Well, I think the important question is how are *you*?"

My father (puzzled): "Ummm, I'm fine?"

My mother: "That's good because there are a whole bunch of people out there who don't think you are fine."

My father: "Oh?"

My mother: "I haven't got the full story yet but I'll let you know when you get home."

She finally got the whole story from one of the mothers. She assured the woman that my father was perfectly fine and that he was *not* shot and he was *not* in the hospital. Then she waited for Diana to come home from school – while fending off more phone calls.

When we three kids got home from school, my mother asked Diana what in the world was she thinking by telling that outrageous story! Diana, knowing full well that she had lied, merely shrugged and told my mother, "I didn't have anything else to share."

Exasperated, my mother let out a sigh. She spent over an hour talking to Diana about telling the truth, how dangerous it was to say things like that when we were living in a very volatile area where war was being waged, that people take things like that very seriously and it is not something to joke about or take lightly. All to no avail. When Diana got stubborn and had her mind made up – *nothing* would change it. She felt she had been ordered – against her wishes – to come up with something for "show and tell." So, she did. If she had not been "forced" to participate, it would not have happened. I don't think she was asked for any other "show and tell" input following that incident.

A Good Day

MY PARENTS made a lot of close friends during our time in Laos. Actually, wherever we went, my parents made friends, many of whom they stay in touch with today. There were many single people we got to know – they were there without family mainly due to the fact that Laos was considered "high risk." At the age of 13, I was pretty ignorant of the volatile political turmoil surrounding us. I think my parents tried hard to protect my sisters and I from the problematic Vietnam War being waged close by.

Diana, George and Michelle

The story I want to relate is actually about one of the single men who my parents befriended. George Kenning, who was in his late 30's, resembled the "dream man" of every young girl – he was incredibly handsome, tall, tan and had these piercing eyes that made you feel as if you were the only one in the room. He was very charming and entranced my sisters and me from the moment we met him (and he still has this ability). He had captured our young hearts, although none of us were bold enough to admit it – until George told us the story about a very special letter.

In 1974, George (my father calls him "Gort" but my sisters and I prefer his given name – it's more sophisticated) was sent to a temporary duty station for 6 months. The assignment was in Cambodia – a war zone. Needless to say, being in the middle of a hostile area where battles were being fought was not a fun time for George or the other CIA officers who were running paramilitary operations. The CIA was sending in "friendlies" on patrol into enemy-held territory to obtain crucial information about the enemy's operations and locations. Then, they had to get these patrols out safely to debrief them for information.

For a while, George was assigned "up country" to a place called Battambong. This was not a pretty place to be. There were good days and bad days and you never knew what kind of day it was going to be when you woke up in the morning. George returned one day from a particularly dangerous "extraction" operation where they had taken enemy gunfire directly into the helicopter. That was definitely considered a *very* "bad day."

When George got back to the command post, thanking his lucky stars that he was still alive, he had some mail waiting for him. Among the various pieces of correspondence he received, there was a hand-written envelope addressed to him from my sister Diana.

Diana was 9 years old at the time. At that age, all children's letters start out pretty much the way their Moms and Dads tell them to write it – and the letters are usually very brief and say the same thing.

Diana's letter fit the standard with one exception. When George opened his letter from Diana, it read:

"Dear George,

How are you? I am fine.

ARE YOU GOING TO MARRY ME OR NOT?

Love, Diana"

With this note, George's bad day ended up a good one.

The Class Play

EVERY YEAR, each class at school put on a play and all the other students attended and rated the performances. My 6th grade class was on the schedule and we had to try and fill up a ½ hour on stage. We made up a play about the travels of a piece of bubblegum, starting from the time of purchase, to being spit on the floor, to ending up on the bottom of someone's shoe, to being scraped off on a sidewalk and so on until the very last person picks it up and starts chewing again. This brought laughs and groans from the audience.

I do remember that the play was not long enough to fill a half hour so we decided to have a "commercial break." I was selected to do the commercial. I went home and asked my mother and father what I should do. My father gave me a wonderful idea. I practiced it in front of my class and they loved it. We kept our play and the commercial a big secret from the rest of the school.

The big day arrived and we were all nervous and excited. Our class was finally announced and we ran up on stage. I waited behind the curtains for the break. I was dressed in a tuxedo and had a fake mustache. When it was time for the commercial, I walked out onto the stage, bringing with me a small table, a plastic bowl, a small box of Cheer laundry soap and a basket with dirty clothes.

I tried to be very dignified as I set up the table and carefully arranged the bowl and the laundry soap. I did all this silently, which was rather nerve-racking since the entire audience was also silent and watching my every move. I took a deep breath and said in a very loud (and shaky) voice: "Ahem. May I have your attention please? I wish to show you the amazing strength and cleaning power of Cheer." I held up the box of Cheer and showed it back and forth to the audience. Then I pretended to pour the laundry powder into the bowl in front of me.

I took the first piece of clothing from the basket at my feet and held it up for everyone to see. "Daddy's shirt," I announced. Then, dipping the shirt in the plastic bowl (which was empty), I pumped the shirt up and down as if scrubbing it and said, "Wishy-washy! Wishy-washy!" Done, I held the shirt up as before and said, "Looks clean!" I sniffed the shirt loudly, "Smells clean!" Then I placed the shirt next to the bowl and proudly finished with, "Is clean!"

Next I held up a woman's nightgown. "Mommy's nightgown." I displayed the item to the audience. I was feeling less nervous so I became a little cockier. I dipped and washed the item as before, repeating my previous actions. "Wishy-washy! Wishy-washy!" I held up the nightgown, "Looks clean!" Sniffed it, "Smells clean!" I gave the audience a big smile and put it down, "Is clean!"

Then I picked up and displayed the final item in the basket. "Baby's diaper." I pretended to wash the item as before, "Wishy-washy! Wishy-washy!" Then, I held the diaper up and said, "Looks clean!" I smelled the diaper deeply and, with my best look of horror and disgust, quickly threw the diaper back in the bowl and washed vehemently again, "Wishy-washy! Wishy-washy!"

The audience roared and loved it. I was voted "Best Commercial," even though that category had not existed before. I was told to go back up on stage for the award and was greeted with more applause. I was beaming with pride. Thanks to my father, I was a "hit!"

The Chemistry Disaster

ONE YEAR I got a chemistry set for Christmas. It had all the cool tools like a microscope, a beaker, test tubes, Petri dishes and stirring utensils. Plus it had all kinds of different solutions and minerals. The set also came with directions on how to make dry ice, grow bacteria and all kinds of other neat stuff.

After playing with it for a few days, I asked to go over to my friend's house to show her my new gift. My father gave me a ride over to Alison's house. She was excited about showing me all her new stuff. We played for a while and then I showed her the chemistry set. She could be a daredevil at times and suggested we try to make a bottle rocket (she'd heard her older brother bragging about making these rockets with his friends). I hesitated only because I knew her parents were extremely strict. In fact, they were not sure they liked me because I was such a tomboy and they thought I was a bad influence on their daughter. Little did they know that many of the pranks and incidents we were involved in were Alison's ideas!

Alison insisted it would be fun and a "learning experience." We found an empty glass bottle and set about making the "rocket." Since the chemistry set did not come with bottle rocket directions (naturally), we decided to mix together just about every solution available in the set. We poured the resulting brown, murky-looking liquid into the bottle and stuffed a rag on the top. Then we started to walk away to look for some matches to light the rag.

Luckily, we had left the glass bottle out on the paved driveway away from the house - because we had not walked more than 10 yards when – *BOOM* – ! The glass bottle exploded into a million chards of glass. Alison and I dived for the ground. It was a good thing we were too far away for the glass to reach us because the damage could have been very severe. As it was, we got into some *serious* trouble.

Alison's father came running as soon as he heard the loud explosion. When he saw we were okay, he walked to the driveway and observed the pieces of glass and burnt rag. Alison and I glanced at each other and exchanged *"we are-really-in-for-it"* looks and waited.

Mr. Emory was not one to mince words nor did he try and keep his voice down. He marched over to where we were standing and stopped directly in front of me. He bellowed at me, *"What did you think you were doing? Do you know how dangerous it is to mess with chemicals? There could have been someone injured or a fire or damage to the house!"* He continued on and on, ranting and raving. He was beet red and had a look of sheer rage on his face that unnerved me. I endured the onslaught silently until he thundered an ultimatum.

Getting to the end of his tirade, Mr. Emory told me I was not welcome at their home anymore. When he said that, I became indignant and tried to interrupt his rampage. I bravely told him that it was *both* our faults, not just mine, but he roared at me to be quiet. Alison said nothing – she just stood there frozen in fear. Then her father grabbed Alison by the arm and hauled her into the house, telling me to "stay put!" Like a shunned sinner, I was not allowed back in the house. I had to wait on the driveway by the gate with my chemistry set while Alison's father called my parents and told them I needed to go home.

When my father arrived, he asked me what happened and I told him the whole story. I also said I didn't think it was fair that the Alison's father was blaming me for the whole thing when it had been Alison's idea in the first place. My father said it sounded like it was both our faults but that I should not have been singled out. He also gave me a shorter and quieter lecture about the dangers of messing with stuff you know nothing about. After that, I saw Alison at school but never went to her house again. Our friendship gradually drifted apart as I started making other friends. But I never forgot the maniacal look on her father's face as he roared at me. It was scary.

The Love Dilemma

IN SIXTH grade, I was just beginning to get interested in the opposite sex. Having always been a tomboy, I was very naïve about boys and "going steady." Of course, there was lots of peer pressure to "have a boyfriend." This kind of pressure makes it difficult to really know who you want for a boyfriend or who might want you for a girlfriend.

I was informed through the "grapevine" that there were two boys who were interested in me and wanted me to be their girlfriend. I was friends with both boys – Randy and Eric. They were both cute but very different. Randy was dark-haired, rowdy and loud. Eric was blond, quiet and more sophisticated. I liked both of them very much and was torn when everything finally culminated in an ultimatum. I had to choose.

I went home and decided to ask my mother what to do. This is when I found out how sometimes it seems that adults know very little about "sixth-grade love," only to discover that my mother had her own intelligent way of handling things. I explained the whole thing to my mother who listened very carefully. Desperate for help, I asked her what I should do. She thought about it and finally said, "Well, if you like them both and can't choose – don't. You're too young to go steady anyway."

Exasperated, I groaned, drawing out the word like a whine, *"Maaawwwm!"* I pouted, "That doesn't help me at all!"

She shook her head, threw up her hands and said, "That's just the way it is, kiddo."

I thought my mother was so wrong until I thought about it later and it hit me that she had actually given me an "out." I went back to school the next day and told both boys that I was "not allowed" to go steady with anyone so we'd all have to remain friends. Not only was I relieved, but I think both of them were too. The problem was solved.

Lucky and Peter

WHILE WE were in Laos, my parents had lots of parties. At my age I only understood that it was what adults did for fun. I found the parties very boring. All grown-ups did was talk, talk, talk. My father likes to tell a story about his friend Brian who came to one of the parties. Brian saw something that made him walk over to my father. Brian told my father that he thought he had better leave because he might have had too much to drink or he was losing his mind. My father said, "But Brian, you just got here."

Brian responded shaking his head, "Yeah – well – I must be either drunk or crazy because – um – I'm a little embarrassed to tell you this – but I *swear* I just saw a white rabbit chasing a little dog across your lawn. I must either be seeing things or hallucinating."

My father laughed heartily at this and told Brian, "No, you're okay. That's Peter, our rabbit. And the dog is Lucky. Peter chases Lucky all the time."

Brian was amazed. "A rabbit chasing a dog? I thought it was supposed to be the other way around."

"Well, you ought to know things are never quite normal at this house."

That story has been told many times by my father because it was true. Lucky would find Peter on the lawn where he was quietly chewing on some grass. Peter would be happy and content until Lucky appeared barking and growling, looking very fierce. Initially, Peter would run away and let Lucky chase him until he ended up in a corner. Peter was then forced to turn and face Lucky who was still barking. Lucky was so little, every time she barked, her whole body lifted slightly off the ground.

Our sweet "Lucky"

Peter (he was a lot bigger than he looks in this picture!)

As soon as Peter was cornered, he would rise up on his hind feet, hissing and spitting angrily. When he did this, you could see that he was a *very* large rabbit. When Peter got pissed off, he was ferocious. Lucky would continue her tirade until, thoroughly enraged, Peter would lunge at her. This is what caused the reverse chase. There were many times when Lucky felt those rabbit teeth snapping at her legs. "She started it – she deserves it," my father would calmly say while watching Lucky run for her life from the snapping, hissing white rabbit.

Holidays and Celebrations

CHRISTMAS WAS an interesting time in Laos. The natural environment of the land did not allow for evergreen trees so my parents purchased a fake one. It turned out to be a terribly complicated and difficult task to put the tree together. Within about 5 minutes of assembly, my father would begin his swearing tirade and tell one of us to go and get him a cold beer.

Our servants were fascinated with this particular holiday. Christmas was not celebrated in Laos so watching my parents put together a fake tree in 90-degree weather and then put presents under it was great entertainment. Dang in particular loved this event. After discovering that some of the packages under the tree had her name on it, she was hooked.

My father took great pleasure in teasing her about which package was hers and what could possibly be in it. But she had to wait for Christmas morning just like we did. None of our help really understood what we were doing or why, but they had great fun participating. It felt strange to celebrate Christmas when it was so hot outside and there was no snow.

The Laotian celebration I remember the best was called "Pi Mai" (pronounced 'pee my'). We used to call it, "The Water Festival." For kids, this was a great holiday. It was held in the early spring and signified a time when the Lao celebrated the rainy season that was about to begin. The rain would bring bountiful crops by summer and fall.

We were told that tossing water on someone was a sign that you were wishing that person a fertile crop and a good rainy season. Thus water also signified a blessing for good fortune and good health. Once we discovered that it was actually okay to throw water on someone, who could resist that?

My sisters and I used to wait by the gate of our house dressed in our swimsuits. We'd have the garden hose out just to drench some poor soul who happened to be walking along the road. My mother would eventually come out and make us return our weapon to the garden although I think she secretly got a kick out of watching our antics.

The other thing I remember is the crazy stuff my father used to do. One time he took my sisters and me out in his old car. Before we left, he filled up the inside of the car with water. Then we drove into town and started throwing the water out of the car with buckets. We were laughing like crazy every time we drove by some surprised Lao civilian and threw out a bucket of water. We felt like we were "Water Queens." I still cannot believe my father did that to his car.

Movies and Parties

ONE THING to remember about where we were living – there was no TV. ("It's good for you – now you have *lots* of time to read," was my mother's motto). The American embassy compound had a movie theatre but we were seldom allowed to go. If we wanted to see a movie, my mother or father had to go to the American commissary and rent a movie camera.

Seeing home movies did not happen too often because my parents would have to lug the entire equipment home, including the big reels of film footage. Then my mother would have to clear one of the walls in the living room where the movie picture would show. Getting to watch a movie at home was a "special treat," and we avidly watched whatever movie was brought home. And we would watch it over and over and *over* again.

At one of my birthday celebrations, my father brought home the James Bond movie, *Live and Let Die*. I can still recall all the scenes and the theme music from that movie. I believe we watched it at least 20 times in three days. You could only keep a movie for a few days because there were lots of other families wanting to see the new movies when they arrived at the commissary. And, in the end, my mother was right. Without the draw of T.V., I read all the time and excelled in reading and writing. My sisters also very quickly picked up good reading skills at a young age.

For his own social outlet, my father had a club where he liked to go and hang out called the "Purple Porpoise." He took me there a few times when we were out and he wanted to stop for a drink. It was a lounge club with a large fully equipped bar, plush red velvet chairs and low, dark tables. It was always very dim and cool inside.

The Purple Porpoise, Vientiane, Laos

I loved going there because the owner, Montegue Banks (we called him "Monty"), knew hundreds of card tricks. I would sit in the soft red chair sipping my ice-cold Coca-cola and Monty would patiently show me how to handle cards. He showed me how to shuffle without mixing in the top or bottom card. He taught me how to shuffle cards in the air without dropping a card.

The different tricks he knew fascinated me. His fingers were quick and he had the "sleight of hand" down to a science. The effect was magical. I was also so curious as to how he could do all these things while unable to even see the cards he was dealing with because he was almost completely blind. When we got home, I would practice the card tricks on my sisters, trying to perfect them the way Monty taught me.

In Laos we went to a lot of parties. I think it was partly because of the nature of my father's job, but also because there was nothing else for the adults to do. I remember one party held at a place close to the Mekong River. It was a brutally hot day and the hosts were cooking a calf over a gigantic pit. It was going to be awhile before we ate so my father told us he'd take us swimming.

Not thinking, we took off our sandals and ran with our towels toward the river. About halfway there, our poor feet were being scorched on the burning, hot sand and there was no shade anywhere. The three of us started screaming at the tops of our lungs. My father grabbed the twins and carried them to the shore. I struggled forward, feet burning horribly, and thankfully made it without blistering. We easily could have burned our feet to the point of needing medical care.

My mother brought our sandals out to us. She was smart and did not remove hers. She was rather displeased with my father for not being more careful. She refrained from saying anything but I saw her give him "The Look." He ignored her and encouraged us to cool our feet in the river.

We swam and played in the river. It turned out to be a rather long day so we spent quite some time in the water. The Mekong River is one of the most filthy and polluted rivers in the world. The Lao people use it for bathing and they also throw their waste and garbage in it. Of course, where we were playing, the water did not seem that bad. We were to find out later that we should *never* have gone swimming in it.

The very next morning after the party, I woke up and found my legs were covered with red dots. I went down to my mother and showed her. There weren't that many and they were only on my legs, so she did not seem too worried. It wasn't until the red dots turned into huge, angry-looking boils that she took me to the medical center. The doctor there lanced the boils and drained them, but told her she would have to continue to drain and monitor them until they completely healed. Left to themselves they could fester and release poison into my bloodstream, which would easily kill me.

My mother was not happy about this messy job. It was disgusting and it was also painful for me. To this day I still

126

have the small scars where the largest of the boils existed. I never stepped foot in the Mekong River after that. Once was all I needed to be taught a lesson about the dangers of polluted water.

Saying Goodbye

WHEN THE war that was going on in Southeast Asia finally came too close for comfort, my father was told that we would be leaving. He was not, however, given a specific date, just a "head's up" to start getting ready. He told my mother that we would probably only be given one or two days notice about the exit date which did *not* make my mother very happy.

We were evacuated in the middle of 1974[*], when the government knew that it would be withdrawing from the war. Once we were informed about the fact that we would be leaving, my mother came and told me that we were going to have to sell Pywaket to someone who could care for him. I was devastated, of course, but my mother explained that if we did not find someone to take him in, he'd most likely be killed and eaten.

We found a Laotian family with a young 10-year old girl who wanted to have a horse and learn how to ride. I was heartbroken when I had to leave him with her. Much to my torment, a whole month went by before we actually left! I missed my horse so much. So, after two weeks of waiting to leave, I went to my mother and asked if I could go and visit Pywaket and see how he was doing with his new family. My mother acquiesced and my father drove me over to their house. He dropped me off and said he'd be back in an hour.

---

[*] Officially, in 1975, in accordance with the Paris Peace Agreement on Indochina of January 27, 1973, the United States withdrew its troops and advisers from Laos, South Vietnam and Cambodia. The North Vietnamese government, took over South Vietnam by invasion with armed forces. The Khmer Rouge regime took over Cambodia. Then the communist Phathet Lao movement, financed and supported by the North Vietnamese and Russian governments, took over Laos by invasion with armed forces and formed the Lao People's Democratic Republic.

I walked toward the house – planning to knock on the door and announce my visit – when I happened to look to my left at their large garden area. There was Pywaket, warily looking at me, and he was so *fat*! I was dumbfounded. He dipped his head and chewed on some more grass and I called his name. He bared his teeth at me and snorted warnings. I could tell that he had not been ridden or exercised *at all* since I had left him there! When a horse is young and does not get enough exercise or discipline, it can become quite wild. I found out later that the girl was too afraid of him and no one else wanted to go near him, so they just let him freely roam around the garden and left food out for him.

Well, I certainly was not going to let this little demon get the best of me. I went and got his bridle – which was still hanging in their garage where I left it – and I walked right up to the snorting, bucking Pywaket. He glared at me and rolled his eyes, trying to look so ferocious. He struggled furiously with me but I got that darn bridle on him. By then the girl's father had come out and explained the situation. I told him I was taking Pywaket out for some exercise. He shrugged his indifference and I jumped on Pywaket and away we went.

We went for a very long, hard ride. Pywaket was sweating and breathing heavily when we got back. My father was waiting for me when I returned. He'd already learned from the girl's father what was happening. The family wanted to be rid of the horse – they said he was uncontrollable and wild. Fortunately, my father was able to find a farmer who was willing to take Pywaket. My father thinks Pywaket ended up living a long life, racing around the fields. I hope so. That's how I want to remember it anyway.

Leaving Laos

TONKEN AND his village wanted to have a farewell party for us to say good-bye. The Lao celebrate life's events with a formal party called a "Baci" (pronounced 'ba-si'). If there is a death in the family, a child is born, a marriage is celebrated or a family is departing the village, there is a Baci thrown for the family.

It is considered a great honor to participate in a Baci celebration. Buddhist monks are invited to come and bring blessings and prayers. People dress in their best clothes and a feast of mouth-watering, enticing foods is prepared. The

My Father and Mother at a Lao Baci

decorations are bright and festive. Some of these celebrations can last all day or even longer. As far as I know, we were one of the very few American families ever given the honor of a Baci.

I remember being overwhelmed at the number of people who came. The event was festive and yet sad because we knew we were saying good-bye. The tables and walls were wonderfully decorated and delicious food was prepared. The custom was for everyone to gather and hear the monks' prayers. The monks dressed in bright orange robes and sat with their shaved heads bowed. The prayers lasted for a long time. The prayers were said in a monotone and they droned on and on. I fidgeted with impatience and my sisters were restless as well, but one "look" from my mother kept us glued to our seats.

Finally, the prayers were over. We were told to stand and then all the guests formed a line. Each person took pieces of thin, white string from a large bowl that the monks had blessed. Then, one by one, they approached us – first my father, then my mother, then my sisters and then me. They tied a piece of string around one of our wrists, bowed their heads and murmured a prayer as they did so. There were many who were in tears because we were leaving. It was very moving. Some of the prayers given to us were to have a happy life, a safe trip, good health or long life.

When every person had given us their individual blessing, our arms were covered in white string. My father says we should consider the wishes we received and the Baci a rare and special honor. After all the blessings were over, it was time for celebration and eating and dancing. It was a great deal of fun although I remember finding it difficult to eat because I could hardly bend my string-covered arms. I think my mother cut some of the string off later that night (that's a "no-no" to the Lao), just so we could do the basics like brush our teeth, go to the bathroom, etc.

A few days later we left. Many people came to the airport to wave good-bye, including Dang and Tonken. There was lots of laughing but much crying as well. I was so sad to go. We kept what was left of the string on our arms for about two weeks. According to my mother, that was long enough. My father once told me you were supposed to keep the string on until it fell off by itself. I think he is right but my mother was not going to be able to handle watching the white string slowly turn black and grimy. I am sure it was hard enough for her to look at it for the two weeks and not run for scissors to cut the offensive, germ-laden strings off.

Before we left, my father – ever the schemer – did not want "the enemy" to have access to the household goods we were leaving behind (furniture, washer, refrigerator, and other miscellaneous items). He told Tonken that he had a plan. My father knew it would greatly benefit Tonken's village to obtain any items they could use for themselves or that they could use to barter for food and other necessities.

My father told Tonken that on the night before we were to leave the country, there was not going to be anyone home and no guards would be at the house. He told Tonken to come with the other village men and empty the house. In other words, my father staged a robbery of our house so that the village would be able to take whatever they wanted to use it or sell it on the black market. Tonken understood my father's wishes completely and the next morning, the house was stripped clean. We were already moved out and headed for the airport, so we did not get to see the barren results. My father was happy that he had done something to help the people we were leaving behind.

Peter, the rabbit, was given to Tonken. He was considered a "prize" rabbit because he had such "virility." I am sure Peter ended up making lots and lots of babies and lived a good life. Ah, to be a rabbit (ha ha). Lucky, our dog, we took with us. She lived until she was 14 or 15 years old. We all loved her dearly but my mother was her favorite. She used to follow my mother everywhere and was always tripping my mother up. Lucky led a happy and fulfilling life and ended up with my mother and father when we returned to the United States for good. Since Lucky's death, my parents have never shown any desire to get another pet.

Paris,
France

1974 – 1977

Getting Acquainted with a New Place

AFTER TWO years in Laos, my father was bleakly looking at a return to the bureaucratic misery of working at Langley, when out of the blue, my father was told by his supervisor that there was a "slot" that needed filling in Paris. It was unfortunate that the availability was caused by the French Government tossing out three American agents who were caught doing something "bad" on French soil – however, it was a lucky break for my father.

After we arrived, until my parents could find a place to live, we had to stay at a hotel in downtown Paris located off the Rue George V – a very "posh" area. My parents were not aware that we were staying in the most costly part of the city and were in for a rude surprise at our first dinner in Paris.

After the long plane trip, a taxi ride and my mother's insistence that we do some unpacking, we were starving. We trooped down the hotel stairs and out the door to a small café on the corner. We ordered what seemed to be a fairly simple meal. My sisters and I had hot dogs, French fries and sodas. My parents had a modest meal of steak and potatoes. I'm sure they had a few drinks as well. What I do recall was what happened when we got the bill. I heard a gasp of horror from my father as he stared at the amount of French franks (the currency used by the French) we owed. I know he quickly converted the amount of the bill in his head to American dollars and realized that for the five us, the bill came to $125! Back then, $125 was equivalent to about $250!

My parents were not planning to spend anywhere near that much because we had to stay in a hotel until we found a place to live. Needless to say, we did not eat another meal in the city for a long time. After that shock, my mother went out and bought food that she could make without the use of an oven – or a kitchen for that matter. We ate lots of peanut butter and jelly sandwiches for the next few weeks.

My parents soon found a house and we moved to a small town called Vaucresson. I was 13; my sisters were 9. It was early September 1974 and it was *cold* - quite different from the 90-degree weather in Laos. France was so completely opposite from Laos that it was difficult to adjust to at first. My initial impression was that the country was austere, bleak and crowded with too many cars, buses and trains. In contrast, Laos was rural and had an elegance of open space. The European décor, the richness and abundance of Paris and its tall, majestic buildings seemed so contrary to the poverty and dismal conditions I had seen in Laos. It was overwhelming.

We moved into an enormous house I called the "French Mansion." I was amazed at the size – it reminded me of the "Adam's Family" house. It was three stories high and the top windows were shaped like towers. The rooms were large with high ceilings. Wooden floors spread throughout the house except for the linoleum floor in the kitchen. The staircase that led from the first floor to the third was designed in an elegant manner with a smooth wooden banister, which circled gently upward. We were *not* allowed to slide down the banister.

It was so cold in the house that first fall season that my mother would go down to the kitchen every morning, turn on the stove, leaving the stove door open, and heat the room. She'd holler up the stairs when it was warm. We would jump out of bed, grab our school clothes and race downstairs and into the warm kitchen to get dressed. Compared to the rest of the frigid house, the warmth and brightness of the kitchen was like heaven.

The house had radiators in each room but they were very old and did not do much to warm up the house. If you stood right next to a radiator, you might get warm but only one side at a time. The minute you walked away, you were cold again. We dressed in so many layers of clothes I am sure people thought we were Eskimos. The other problem with the radiators was that steam would build up so it was a good idea to be careful not to turn it on without letting some of the pressure out.

One time I turned on the radiator in my room to get the heat going. About 15 minutes later I remembered I had not opened the spout to let the pressure out. I ran over and turned the knob. There was a loud *"POOF!"* and a spray of hot water shot straight out of the radiator, drenching the wall, the floor and me. Shocked, I shrieked and jumped back. Fortunately my mother did not hear this particular scream, which saved me from getting her "Exasperated Look." My mother was in constant fear that one of the radiators would blow up. Not a pleasant thought in a house made almost entirely of wood. I tried to be more "radiator-friendly" after that episode.

Vaucresson was an attractive town – picturesque and quaint. On many weekends, my father would take us on a walk into town for breakfast, leaving my mother with some peace and quiet in the morning. We would walk several blocks until we got to a steep hill where there was a short-cut and a small path through the neighborhood into town.

It took us about 10 minutes to walk to our favorite bakery. It was always nice and warm inside the store and filled with the most enticing smells. My father let us get whatever we wanted. We'd sit in the bakery and eat our pastries. If it was nice outside, we would sit in the sun and bask in the heat. I always ordered a hot chocolate drink and a "Pain au Chocolat." This was a wonderful, tasty rolled croissant with melted dark chocolate on the inside. Full and satiated, we'd walk back home having spent a relaxing morning with my father.

We could hardly have lived in a safer neighborhood. Around the corner from our house was the French Motorcycle Riot

Police. They were the "muscle" called out to quell riots or manage crowds. Every so often we would hear the sirens and watch as the tall, iron gates opened. A large convoy of motorcycle police on their black motorcycles and shiny helmets would race by, followed by a few police cars with sirens roaring. It was quite impressive and very exciting. It also made us feel a little safer knowing they were right around the corner.

Halloween

OUR HOUSE had a large, dark basement. There were stone steps that circled downward and the further down you went, the darker and gloomier it got. The basement was made completely of cement with hard, cold floors. There were several rooms that looked like they had been chiseled out of the foundation. My father fixed up one room as a place where he could put his tools and his dartboard. Another room contained the washer and dryer. The other two rooms were further into the basement. These rooms were very dark and eerie. My father kept chopped wood and his axe in one of the rooms. The other we used as a storage area for our skis, boots, sleds, Christmas stuff, bikes, etc. The whole basement was a creepy place and only dimly lit with a few swinging light bulbs.

We used to have Halloween parties and set the basement up as the "haunted house" area. We scared all the kids who dared come down into the "dungeon." The washroom was

set up as the "ghost" or "witch" room. When the kids ventured in, I would swing a white sheet shaped as a ghost or a black witch figure at them. At the same time, I would pull open the dryer door that was set to make a loud buzzing sound.

The younger kids never got past this room. They'd be running up the stairs screaming by then.

When the older kids were able to survive this room, the next step was to lead them down to the "axe" room where my father would be waiting, grinning like a ghoul. I would tell them a story about a crazy man who was found in this house, locked in this very basement room for many, many years. As soon as my father heard me telling the story, he would begin chopping wood very slowly.

While the kids were listening to me describe the psychopath who was found covered in blood, surrounded by skulls and newly cleaved bodies, my father would systematically chop wood, the sound getting louder as we approached. *Chop, chop, CHOP!* My father could make the most horrible sounds and if the kids had not fled by now, my father would let out a bloodcurdling howl and then laugh and laugh like a crazy man. Inevitably, this led to a flurry of screams and fleeing children, leaving me in the basement with my father, chuckling at our success. This stuff was our forte.

Entertainment and Television

MY PARENTS had huge barbeque parties while we lived in France, and all our Lao friends (some that we had helped get out of Laos) would come and put their skills at Laotian cooking to the test. We loved it when our Lao friends came over because the dishes they cooked up and served were so delicious.

There was "sticky rice" served with different sauces – from sweet to very spicy. There were spring rolls and lettuce-wrapped appetizers. There was a huge pot of Hot and Sour soup that smelled delicious while it cooked on the stove. And there was lots of fresh cooked pork and beef. My mouth waters when I think of all the delicious foods we had. The parties could get very rowdy and loud. As I got older, my parents entrusted me to help with serving drinks and food. I always had a good time helping out.

For entertainment, other than my parent's parties, sometimes my mother allowed us to watch television. After school, my sisters and I would sit down and watch some of the afternoon shows. These were all in the French language, naturally. It was amusing to watch "Wild Wild West" and "Star Trek" with the characters all speaking in French. The shows were dubbed, of course. Whoever was in charge of changing the language from English to French was not very good at it. Half the time you would see Captain Kirk say, "Ready for Warp Power ... Now!" with his lips and then the French translation, "Attention! Varp Energie ... tout suite!" The translation was always a few seconds slow which made us laugh. Although everything on T.V. was in French, at least here we had television!

Our First Christmas

MY MOTHER'S fondest memory of Christmas is the one we celebrated our first year in Paris. A few days before Christmas Eve, my parents went out and bought a huge Christmas tree – it was so high it touched the ceiling and it was very, very full. As soon as my father brought it in the house, we could smell the sweet scent of pine, bringing the thought of Christmas and Santa Clause very much to mind.

My mother was impatiently awaiting several of our boxes that had still not arrived since our move – they were misplaced or lost – and one of them was full of all the ornaments and lights and everything a Christmas tree needs to be decorated. She did not want to go out and buy a bunch of stuff because then we'd have way too many decorations and lights. She wanted to dress the tree with all the ornaments she and my father had collected over the years. So, we waited. The three of us children were particularly anxious about the tree because what would Santa think if he arrived and there was nothing on the tree? Plus how would he find us so far away without all our "stuff" hanging where it was supposed to be?

Christmas Eve arrived and my mother reluctantly had to admit that we were not going to get our box of Christmas decorations. She told us that it was going to be up to the three of us to decorate the tree with whatever we had. She presented her ideas to a trio of doubting, crestfallen faces. She told us we would make popcorn strings and wind them around the tree like they were lights. We'd bake tons of cookies and decorate them with different colored icing to add color to the tree. And, we were to go out into the garden and search for pinecones.

After she described our activities for the day, we were renewed with hope. We enthusiastically threw ourselves into the various activities with my mother as director. She popped immense amounts of popcorn. She made cookie dough and had the twins cut cookies in Christmas shapes. The kitchen floor was soon covered with popcorn and cookie crumbs. The kitchen table was also a gigantic mess of flour, icing and cookie dough. On this day my mother was unusually tolerant of the disarray.

Stringing the popcorn took a long time, especially for such a large tree, but I was determined to make this tree beautiful and festive. My father monitored how much icing was getting onto the cookies to keep it from ending up in twins' stomachs. In the end, we managed to produce quite a large crop of decorated "ornaments."

The fun part was when we actually decorated the tree. My father built a great big roaring fire in the fireplace in the room across from the tree. We put on our Andy Williams Christmas Carol tape (my absolute favorite Christmas tape to this day) and played the music loud. My father got a ladder and wound the popcorn strings all around the tree. The twins hung cookie ornaments as high as their arms would let them (we later moved many of the lower-hanging cookies up onto the higher branches. They were doing such a good job, we couldn't tell them to do any different). We all sang Christmas carols with 'Andy' and placed the pinecones we'd found all throughout the tree. I went upstairs and found some small stuffed animals and we put those on some empty branches. It was a wonderful, festive time.

Finally, my mother declared the tree "done." In spite of having been deprived of our box of "real" Christmas stuff, we had managed to create a magnificent Christmas tree. My mother says that she thinks it is the best tree we ever had. We also started a family tradition that night. We realized how much fun it was to decorate the tree on Christmas Eve, so it became a family custom to have a party and decorate the tree at that special time.

When we celebrated Christmas during our second year in Paris, we received an extra-special gift from our cousin Sashy. She was about four years old at the time and sent us a present all the way from Los Angeles.

That Christmas morning, as we opened up our gifts, my father saw a package addressed in a child's handwriting. Curious, he opened it and started laughing. We all watched as he lifted out a Christmas ornament that Sashy had made herself. It was a snowman made out of a stack of three Styrofoam balls stuck together in layers. It had little black eyes, a red nose and arms made out of Popsicle sticks. The only problem was that Sashy had painted it a dark brown so you can imagine what it resembled. Chuckling, my father held it out for us to admire and then said, "So what shall we call this little guy?" He paused, thinking, and then said, "Hey – how about – '*The Doo-Doo Man*?'"

Well that busted us all up and the name stuck. I believe my parents still own 'The Doo-Doo Man' and religiously put it on the Christmas tree every year. We waited many years before reminding Sashy about her infamous and funny gift, and then of course telling her what we named her "snowman."

Babysitting the Manning Kids

I STARTED babysitting for the Manning family fairly soon after our arrival in France. In fact, my introduction to the Manning family happened to be on the day after Christmas. Since I'd been taking care of my sisters for a long time, and I was now 13 years old, my mother figured I was responsible enough to baby-sit other children. I was excited about the prospect of actually being old enough to earn some money.

Mr. Manning was an executive with IBM and had been with the company for many years. He and his wife had two older children who were living on their own in the United States and going to school. The two older siblings used to come and visit on holidays. After their second child was born, 10 years passed and suddenly the Manning's decided to have two more children. Diane was 7 when I started babysitting – David had just turned 3.

I'll never forget the first night I arrived at the Manning's house. Mrs. Manning was elegantly dressed and Mr. Manning was wearing a tuxedo. David was screaming and hanging onto his mother's leg, saying he did not want her to leave. He was a solid little boy, blond and cute as a button, and he was very used to getting his way. He shouted – enraged – and began hitting his mother in the stomach. I was shocked that she let this behavior happen. Ten seconds with *my* mother and this child would know what the word "discipline" meant. As the tirade went on, Mrs. Manning looked at me helplessly. I bent down to the red-faced, angry little boy and said, "Hey, David. My name is Leigh. I'm the new babysitter. Want to play some games?"

Distracted for a moment, he let go of his mother who moved quickly away. Mr. Manning was helping her on with her coat when David, a look of rage combined with a glint of intelligent knowledge in his eyes, ran over to me and lifted his foot back – ready to launch a kick at my shin. I looked right at him and said, "David, if you kick me, I am going to kick you right back."

He smiled with a knowing look. He knew his status in the house was so high that he was untouchable. The little brat kicked me hard on the shin. Then he stood back and looked at me in defiance. That was it for me. I said, "Well, buddy, you did it now." I kicked him back on his little shin. I knew I had not kicked hard enough to cause any pain, but he began to wail like I had scorched his skin with a hot iron.

Mr. and Mrs. Manning stood there staring at me like I was some kind of alien. I told them, "Oh, don't worry about it. I have two little sisters who were just like him when they were his age. He and I will be friends before you know it." I tried to grab David but he ran screaming down the hall as if I were the devil herself.

All through this, his sister Diane had stood quietly watching. When I turned to her, I saw an amused smile on her face and a look of wonder. I guess no one had ever done that to her little brother before. The Mannings quickly left, hesitating briefly at the door (probably wondering if their children would survive the night) and then they were gone.

I smiled at Diane and asked her to give me a tour of the house. I could see from the hallway that the house was huge. Diane led me past the dining room. I admired the antique oak dining room table on top of which stood two beautiful, silver candlesticks. The room had a majestic look to it. There were flowers in silver bowls on either end of the matching armoires along the wall. Next to the dining room was the main living room, which was very bright and lined with beautiful, soft white sofas and colorful pillows. The Christmas tree was in the living room. It was huge and covered with sparkling lights and decorations.

My appreciation of the décor was distracted, however, by the enormous mass of wrapping paper, boxes, gifts, toys, and clothes which were strewn all over the rug. I could not even see what color the rug was, it was so covered in the aftermath of Christmas debris! I was amazed that people would leave their house looking like this. I shook my head in wonder and followed Diane as she then led me down a narrow hall to the bedrooms. The master bedroom was beautiful – very clean and organized. David's room, however, was a complete mess with clothes and toys all over the place. Diane's room wasn't as bad but definitely needed some kind of organization. David was hiding in his room somewhere but I made no attempt to find him or persuade him to come out. I already had my plan in mind. I knew how to entice kids.

I told Diane we were going to play a game but first I needed three big boxes. We went into the living room and found three decent size boxes. I explained to her that we were going to be in a race – contestants against each other. The trick was that we had to go through the room as fast as we could and pick up everything. All the wrapping paper, ribbons and other garbage was to go into box #1, Diane's toys and clothes went into box #2 and anything that was David's went into the third.

Every time one of us put something in the box, we were to yell, "Score!" or "Basket!" Whoever finished first was the winner. I also told her that if the wrong toy went in the wrong box, that could mean disqualification. I asked her if she was ready. Her eyes were all aglow with the challenge. She nodded and I yelled, "*Go!*" at the top of my lungs (I knew David would hear this. He'd already crept out of his room and was watching from the dark hallway).

The game turned out to be really fun. Wrapping paper and ribbons and toys were flying. We were running around throwing stuff, laughing and yelling, "Score!" and "I just made a basket!" As we neared the end – I was planning on letting Diane win – I saw David. He had come all the way from the hall to the edge of the living room carpet and was watching, enthralled.

Finally, we were down to the last of the toys. I was holding one of the numerous trucks I'd found, getting ready to toss it into the #3 box when Diane finished first, throwing a doll enthusiastically into her box. She yelled, "I won! I won!" and danced around the room, her arms raised overhead like a runner who'd just won a gold medal. I clapped and cheered. And guess what? The room was clean! Hallelujah!

Suddenly David got up and ran to his box, throwing toys out of it saying, "I wanna play! I wanna play!" I immediately stopped him and made him look at me. I told him the garbage was staying in its box and going into the garage for his daddy to put away but that we could empty his and Diane's box, mix the toys up and play the race *one time* only. Then, I told him, I had another really fun game to play. I rolled my eyes at Diane about having to play the same game again, but she was a real trooper and understood a great deal for her age.

I tired them out that first night. We cleaned the living room, straightened out their rooms (I made it fun), and played a game similar to "Hide-and-Seek" which I called "Cowboys and Indians." This game was the cincher for making sure they both slept like the dead. It was like the game I played with my sisters in Laos, but here we had the bedrooms and hallway areas to play in. It could get pretty wild with all three of us whooping it up and down the halls. It turned out to be one of David's favorite games (all little boys like "shoot-em-ups") and it became one of my most effective "behavior" bribes.

After all the evening's activities, it was obvious I had managed to drain all the energy from their little bodies. I got them ready for bed with baths and PJ's. Then I started to read David a story. He fell asleep before I had turned the first page. I sat down with Diane and started to read a long story.

I promised that every time I babysat, we'd read some more. Satisfied, she too was quickly asleep. I had let them stay up a little later than I usually would, but I knew they'd been cooped up in the house too long.

After making sure they were fast asleep, I finished straightening the living room and went into the kitchen. I washed all, the dishes that were in the sink and on the counters. Then I dried the dishes and put everything away. After the kitchen was clean, I grabbed a snack and a soda. I settled in the living room in one of the comfy chairs and read my book. I too quickly fell asleep. I was exhausted as well.

A little after one in the morning, the Mannings came home and I woke up when I heard their gasps of surprise. Mrs. Manning was standing in the living room with her mouth open. She looked at me with awe and asked what happened. I grinned and told her we did a little clean up and then played some games and cleaned their rooms. She sputtered a little and said, "You – you – you mean you did all this and they did it with you?"

I said, "Yep, even David and we had a blast. I also made them take baths because we played for a long time and they needed them."

"Baths –?" she stuttered, "and – and cleaned their rooms – ?"

I nodded. Mrs. Manning came over to me and hugged me so tight. "You are amazing," she breathed into my hair. "*Amazing!*"

Mr. Manning asked me if I was ready to go home and I nodded. Mrs. Manning reached into her purse and paid me not only my hourly rate ($2.00) but also gave me a huge bonus amount ("huge" for back then) – I think it was $10. I was thrilled. I thanked her and Mr. Manning. In the car on the way home, Mr. Manning reiterated what his wife had said and told me I was wonderful. He thanked me for all my help and for the clean up of the mountain of Christmas stuff.

After that, I could do no wrong in the eyes of the Mannings. I was their "Number One" babysitter and they constantly requested my services. I was over at the Mannings most weekends after that. They even asked my mother if she would allow me to take care of their David and Diane when they went away for weekend trips. My mother knew I could always call home if there was a problem. I guess you could say I became a "regular" at the Mannings house. It was like having a second family In fact, my mother told me that she spoke to Mrs. Manning years after both David and I were adults and Mrs. Manning told her that David still remembers me as his most favorite babysitter.

Cousin John

MY RESPONSIBILITIES extended beyond babysitting during our stay in Paris. My parents thought I was also a wonderful "tour guide" when we had visitors. Most of our guests appreciated my efforts at showing them the famous sights of Paris, however, one memorable visitor was not so impressed.

My cousin John came for a short visit during spring break one year. John reminds me of my father because he can always make me laugh. He is always clowning around. When he came to visit, he was my age – 14 – and had a "devil-may-care" attitude that immediately became apparent. I think John's parents sent him to France hoping he would appreciate being exposed to a new culture and perhaps soak up some of the sophistication of Paris. Ha! Naturally, my parents were happy to give me the responsibility of "taking care" of my cousin and making sure he got the full tour of Paris. My cousin and I usually got along quite well – as long as he behaved himself.

Our first adventure was at the most famous monument in Paris: The Eiffel Tower. The Eiffel Tower was built between 1887 and 1889. It took 2 years, 2 months and 5 days to complete. It was built for the Universal Exhibition in celebration of the French Revolution. The Tower is almost ¼ mile tall (1,063 feet). It has three stories and if you want to walk up the Tower instead of taking the elevator, you will have to climb 1,665 steps. For comparison sake, the Empire State Building is only a little taller than the Eiffel Tower at 1,454 feet and has 1,860 steps. This was important information that I conveyed to my cousin as we rode the train from Vaucresson into Paris.

John was not really all that interested in all this information, but he was impressed with the Tower itself. It was a cool, crisp spring day and the sun was out although the air was very chilly. We took the elevator to the second tier. There were a few other tourists walking around, admiring the view. In those days, there were no nets hung around the railings. It was very open and quite thrilling to be up so high. You could actually lean over the railing and look directly below to the tiny people and cars and the splendid park.

After a few minutes of admiring the view, John – being John – wanted to go to the very top. Due to the high winds, there were many days when the third story of the Tower was off limits. On this particular day I could see it was closed as indicated by a large "Ferme" sign (meaning "closed") hanging on a thick rope, cordoning off the stairs leading up to the top. But was a small thing like a rope and sign going to stop my headstrong, stubborn cousin? *Of course not.*

John jumped over the rope and started up the stairs while I stood below gesturing at him, "Come back here you *idiot!*" I had just gone through my second attempt at hissing at my cousin when around the corner came the guard who was in charge of the elevator and visitor safety. The guard saw me and began walking over. I tried to whisper to John out of the side of my mouth while simultaneously smiling at the guard. The guard peered up the stairs and saw John. The guard began jabbering in French, pointing and motioning for John to come back down. With a shrug of his shoulders and a big goofy grin, John strolled back down the steps. The guard, not happy with this "American attitude," told us we would have to leave.

I did not feel like waiting for the elevator with an incensed guard so I told John we'd be taking the stairs down. John seemed fine with this decision until we started down. He suddenly realized just how high up we were and that there were lots and lots and *lots* of steps to walk down. That's when the moaning and grumbling and groaning began. I could hear him muttering behind me as we trudged down step after step. It was a very long way. It wasn't exactly the 1,665 steps (since we were not descending from the very top) but it was probably close to maybe 1,300 steps and that's plenty. It took us a long time to get down. Whenever John would fall silent behind me, I would cheerfully say, "Hey, John – you havin' fun yet?" Oh, that would make him so mad and the groaning and mutterings would start all over again. I would chuckle with amusement. Served him right. He's the one that got us into that mess!

Our next adventure in the beautiful city of Paris was to visit the Avenue de Champs Elysées and the famous "Arc De Triomphe[*]." We started out at the bottom of the Champs Elysees and stopped in at several shops. I was actually looking for something for my mother for her birthday. At the first few stores, everything was fine, however, eventually

---

[*] Located at the end of the Champs Elysées, a broad avenue in Paris, is l'Arc de Triomphe (The Arch of Triumph). L'Arc de Triomphe is the largest triumphal arch in the world. It commemorates Napoleon Bonaparte's many victories. Like La Tour Eiffel, it is a symbol of France as well.

John demonstrated that he was getting quite bored with window-shopping.

I was in a store and walking down one of the aisles with John behind me when I heard funny noises. I turned to see John knocking items off the shelf onto the floor. I was shocked and a little annoyed. I told him to watch out and pick up the stuff. That's when he started to make these grunting noises and I looked at his face. He had his eyes rolling all around in his head, he was shrugging one shoulder up and down as if he had a tick and he was drooling. Then he shuffled forward and made some more grunting sounds. I said, "John! What are you *doing*?" He did not answer. Instead he gave me a little smirk and continued with his "mentally disabled" act. I turned around and started back down the aisle saying, "John, knock it off right now. That's *not* funny." He followed after me making "Argh-argh" sounds. He was letting the drool run down his chin! I was disgusted and so *irritated* with him. I turned again and said firmly, "I'm going to the checkout now so you need to straighten up!"

Instead of behaving himself, he kept following me, acting like he was retarded. I kept muttering at him to *"Stop it,"* until I got to the checkout counter. John kept pawing my arm, rolling his eyes and acting like he was trying to say my name: "Lllleeeeeuuuuu. Lllleeeeeuuuu." I finally snapped at him and yelled, "John! Knock it off *right now*!"

I actually heard him muffle a laugh before he continued with the act and now other people in the store, including the shop manager, were looking at me like I was a bad person for mistreating this obviously mentally impaired boy. I kept shaking my head and hissing at John but he continued on with his act wholeheartedly. Finally, we got out of there and as we reached the sidewalk, John was doubled over with laughter. I was so *mad* at him. I punched him as hard as I could on the arm. He kept howling in laughter. Finally, I started to giggle with him. I am sure the people in the store thought I was a horrible caretaker for this poor, defenseless boy.

I decided it was not a good idea to do anymore shopping so we headed directly for the Arc De Triumph – it was about 5 blocks up the street. Because it is such an awesome monument, the Arc is extremely well-known. When John and I exited the store, we could see the Arc clearly from where we were on the sidewalk. But John was not finished with embarrassing me. He started stopping the French people who were walking along, enjoying their spring day. He would run up and ask the person in a desperate manner and with a very strong American accent, "D'ya know where the Arch of Tri-ump is?" The poor person (victim) would look at John, bewildered, and turn and point to the Arc just up the street and say, "C'est la" (It's there).

John would then turn and look at the Arc like he'd never seen it before and gasp, "Oh! Why ain't that somethin'. That

is it! Hey, thanks, man!" I would just keep walking with my

head lowered and my eyes averted from my birdbrain cousin. The terrible part was that he kept doing this all the way up the street. I finally lost my temper when we were actually standing *right under* the Arc and John asked some poor soul there where the Arc was. This person said nothing and backed away from him like he was some kind of alien. I was feeling that exact same way. I could not believe I had been given the unfortunate responsibility of ushering this crazy cousin around. I sighed and told John it was time to go. I wanted to avoid any other confrontations with the French who can often be very feisty people.

After a few more ventures into the city, and receiving absolutely no sympathy from my parents as I recounted John's behavior, I opted for more conventional and athletic activities such as bike riding and exploring the town of Vaucresson. As long as I kept him occupied and active (and away from the French people), everything was fine. I think he had a good time. The last time I spoke with him, he'd forgotten the tormenting he'd done to me. He thought it was still very funny after hearing my description of his antics. "Sounds like something I'd do," he told me.

Trip to Loch Ness Lake

THE SUMMER after I turned 15, my father told my mother he was not going to be able to accompany us on our planned camping trip to the Loch Ness Lake[*] in Scotland. We were planning to drive from campground to campground and view the incredible sights of the mountains and castles and ruins along the way. One of my most favorite things to do was to walk through the ruins of old castles and imagine what had gone on in the olden days.

My mother wanted to do the camping trip anyway, but my father would not hear of her traveling alone with three young girls. That is how we were introduced to Milo. My father brought Milo home one day and told my mother that he would be accompanying us on our trip across Europe. Milo was a short, stocky man with a big head of dark hair and a reddish beard. He was not a handsome man but he was very friendly and talkative. He loved to tell stories and tried to be funny. To this day I do not know how my father talked him into going with us or even why my mother finally acquiesced. I do know my parents argued about it quite a bit until it was time to go.

The day we were to leave, Milo showed up driving a van. After we were done packing, the van looked like it was loaded with enough stuff to house several families. Faced with very few options about what to do, I guess my mother just figured she had no choice if she wanted to have us entertained for most of the summer.

Milo and my father had carefully planned out the trip with maps and big 'X' marks for the places we were going to stay.

---

[*] Loch Ness, the largest freshwater lake in the British Isles, is twenty four miles long and, at one point, one and a half miles wide. It has an average depth of four hundred and fifty feet and at times plunges close to a thousand. It is cold and murky, with dangerous currents. In short, it is the perfect place to hide a monster from even the most prying eyes of science.

Every time we arrived at a campground, we were not allowed to go anywhere until the van was unpacked and the tents were up. Only then were we allowed to go and explore. My mother would begin cooking dinner and when we returned, it was usually dark. We'd sit around a blazing fire and Milo would tell these horrible jokes that my mother never laughed at. Milo's jokes and stories always went on and on and *on*. My mother would sit, waiting for the punch line or the end of the tale – which never seemed to happen. Talk about driving someone crazy. Clenching her teeth, my mother would ask Milo if he was getting to *the point*. He would look at her and give her this big, disarming smile and tell her he was almost there. Be patient. She would sigh and sit in tortured silence.

When it was bedtime, we got into our "commando-suits." My mother – in an effort to find something warm for us to wear because it got very cold at night – had found these nice, thick, comfortable jumpsuit-type pajamas. The only color they came in was black so when we wore these at night, the three of us looked like we were Ninja soldiers preparing for battle. But she was right. We needed them and they kept us toasty warm.

The real problem happened every night at bedtime. There were only two tents. We had brought a three-man tent and a two-man tent. So, *someone* had to sleep with Milo because my mother certainly was not going to share a tent with him! And I was certainly not going to be sleeping in the same tent with a strange man – I was a teenager! So, we'd look at the twins. Michelle, who was bigger than Diana and more verbal, protested vehemently about having to sleep with Milo so it was always Diana who ended up in the two-man tent. To this day Diana never lets us forget the sacrifices she made on our behalf.

I was responsible for making breakfast. I learned how to make scrambled eggs in a skillet over a fire and got quite adept at it. I could even cook bacon. Cleaning the pan was another story. I hated that chore. After breakfast we had to pack everything up, take down the tents and pack the van. It was tedious and time-consuming because Milo (who was usually "Mr. Easy-Going") was extremely picky about how everything was tied down and whether it was packed correctly. After we were done, he'd inspect the van and inevitably would find some minor flaw in our work and have to fix it. My mother would sigh and turn away in exasperation, but there was no moving Milo along any faster or any differently. This was the way it was done and that was that. When I look back and think about how that man had to deal with four females day in and day out for weeks on end – you really have to admire him.

At one campground in England, I made friends with one of the local English girls. Her family stayed in the campground all summer and had a trailer. She invited me for lunch one day. I met her mother who was a large woman, dressed in a flowered dress and an apron. She had a friendly, open face.

As I was sitting in the trailer waiting for lunch, the woman noticed my mother walking by and asked me in her thick English accent, "Is that yer Mum?" I looked out the window and nodded. Then she surprised me by saying, "You know, your Mum walks like a queen." I had never had anyone say that to me before and I felt a rush of pride and admiration for my mother.

Although I said nothing, inside I agreed. My mother does walk like a queen. She has an elegance and poise that makes her stand out. I never forgot that moment. I was also thankful that Milo did not walk by because I was sure the girl's mother would ask if that was "Me Pa," and I did not want to have to answer that question. If I said yes, it was a lie. If I said no, it looked pretty bad for my mother to be traveling with another man. So, I avoided that question as much as I could. My mother says that she was amazed that we never asked her what to say if people asked us who Milo was. I guess we knew not to say too much.

One afternoon as we were driving through England, it started to rain. Milo was driving and as the storm increased in intensity, my mother told Milo we should find a hotel to stay the night. We were somewhere outside of Edinburgh where there was a campsite but my mother did not want to have to put up tents in a downpour. Plus it was very cold. As it got darker and the rain was not letting up, I sensed that my mother was getting worried. We were driving through some very rural areas and there did not appear to be any inns or lodges around.

Finally, Milo drove into a tiny town – by this time we were all starving – and there was a small lodge. After finding a suitable parking spot, we got out and ran to the lodge. We were soaked by the time we got in. The hostess was not pleased at the group of bedraggled strangers. She was very stiff and stern when my mother explained we needed two rooms – not just one – and that we wanted something to eat. The dinner hour was long over but I guess the woman took pity on us because we were escorted to a long table.

We were all unhappy. My mother was upset, hungry and angry about the situation. My sisters and I were drenched, starving and freezing. As Milo looked at us, he told us he was reminded of a joke. We all groaned. My mother told him no one was in the mood, but he just gave her his "Milo-Smile," (which now instantly drove my mother batty) and began. He had a captive audience so there was not much we could do except listen.

Milo began: "There was this man who went to an English restaurant and ordered a bowl of soup. The waiter brought him the soup and the man tasted it and asked the waiter, 'What kind of soup is this?' The waiter replied in his thick English accent, 'Why, it's *bean* soup, sir.' The man looked at the waiter and said, 'Well, I don't care what it's *been*, I want to know what it is now!'"

There was silence around the table and Milo gave us a big grin and then spread his hands as if to say, 'that's it.' I think we were in shock because a few beats of time passed before we got the joke and started laughing. My mother was doubled over. We were howling, holding our stomachs and struggling to stay seated in our chairs. Not only was it a stupid joke, but it was also the *shortest* joke Milo had ever told!

Milo was terribly proud that he was such a hit. He even kept it up when the hostess brought out hot bowls of soup. Milo politely asked what kind of soup it was and whether it was *'bean'* soup. We all lost it again. The stony-faced hostess was not pleased at the raucous laughter that we were unable to control. It turned out to be vegetable beef soup and it tasted wonderful.

When we finally made it to the Loch Ness Lake, we were thrilled. We were sure we were going to see the Loch Ness Monster[*]. My father was finally able to leave work and came and met us at the campground. He was able to spend the rest of our vacation with us. Best of all, *nobody* had to sleep with Milo because (at the specific request of my mother when she called my father from time to time during our travels) my father had brought with him a one-man tent just for Milo! What a relief that was – especially for Diana!

---

[*] Many lakes of Northern Scotland had ancient legends about monsters and the like. In 565 A.D., though, Loch Ness's story was written down. The account tells of Saint Columba who saved a swimmer from a hungry lake monster. From then on rumors about the creature were repeated from time to time. "Nessie" has been described as a creature with "a long, tapering neck, about 6 feet long, and a smallish head with a serpentine look about it, and a huge hump behind..." The length of the monster has been estimated at about thirty feet. Efforts have been made and continue to be made to find the monster but to date, there has been no real hard-core evidence of its existence.

Milo and my father at our campsite at the Loch Ness Lake (note one of the twins in the background with her "Commando-suit" on)

We had such a good time at the Loch Ness. My father brought out an inflatable rubber raft and we watched as he paddled out and began clowning around. The Loch Ness Lake has the *coldest* water. We stayed close to shore where the water was a little warmer, but it was also so murky you could not even see your hand when you submerged it under the water. So, when my father paddled further and further out into the lake and then started jumping around, we were riveted to see if he would fall in – and fall in he did. He popped out of that water so fast it was like he was a jack-in-the-box! We were rolling on the ground laughing. He quickly paddled back and demanded a towel. The water was absolutely freezing.

While we were at the lake, my sisters and I were determined to see 'The Monster.' My mother would announce bedtime and we would go to our tents but then I would rally my sisters and we'd sneak out to see if the monster was rising. Inevitably, my sisters, who were terrified that the monster really would come out and get them, would scream that they saw *'The Monster!'*

My mother, now incensed, would give me that, *'Get-back-to-bed-right-now'* look. I am sure our camping neighbors did not appreciate the screams of terror from the twins. I had myself convinced one night that I saw the monster and my sisters still attest that we did, indeed, see the famous monster. As time passes, I'm no longer so sure – overactive imagination probably. But it was sure fun trying.

The Infamous Yugoslavia Ski Trip

WE RETURNED to our favorite place - St Oswald - for a ski trip. The instructors we'd had when we were stationed in Austria were still there. I was happy that we would be skiing with Armin again. When we saw him, he looked unchanged except for the silver in his hair. He was still tall, tan and handsome and remained enthralled with my mother. He told her often that if she decided she no longer wanted to be with my father, she always had a place to go. I am sure my mother was flattered.

Armin wanted to do something special for my parents. He arranged to take his "class" to ski the mountains in Yugoslavia. This communist country was a place where someone like my father should think twice about entering - given his profession. Armin, of course, did not know that my father was a spy and did not think that taking Americans across the border would be a problem. When he included me in the group, I was very excited. He also invited a Dutch couple from his current ski class to accompany us to make it look more like a "ski class" tour. The twins were handed over to another ski instructor, Günter, who agreed to baby-sit. The trip was going to be a long one. We were to leave early and would not return until late.

We loaded into Armin's van and left in the wee hours of the morning. He had arranged for his brother to do the driving. It was a beautiful winter day – crisp, cold and sunny. We drove for a long time, headed to a place called Kranska Gora. This spot was located in Slovenia, about 45 minutes from the Yugoslavia-Austria border. The high mountain pass crossing was little known except to locals and was called Loibilpass.

After crossing the border, we drove and drove for what seemed forever up this huge mountain until we reached the place Armin was looking for. We got out and he told us to get our skis and put on our ski boots. He pointed to the top of the mountain, which looked terribly far away, and told us we'd be hiking to the top. Hiking and wearing our heavy, awkward ski boots. *Ugh.* But we had no choice. Armin had already started off.

Half an hour of huffing and puffing brought us to the top. The view was stunning. The sky was a deep blue – not a cloud to be seen. The snow stretched out before us like a white ocean, gleaming in the sun. We would be "breaking ground" as Armin put it (only he said it in German). There was not a mark on the clean, white snow.

Our Ski Group – Armin is on the far right; I am next to my mother on the far left

Armin started off and led the way - the rest of us following like obedient children. I liked to be right behind Armin and follow his form and tracks as perfectly as I could. The snow was smooth with just a fine, thin crust that made a light crackling sound as we broke through. It was about 4-5 inches deep. The one thing I remember most clearly is how quiet it was. The only sounds were our skis swooshing through the virgin snow. It was incredible that we were the only ones skiing on the mountain. We were so used to the ski slopes that were more and more packed with people. This was heaven compared to the ski resort. And we did not have to worry about lifts or lines. It was going to take us all day just to get down this mountain.

It was close to mid-morning when we started out and soon it was nearing lunchtime. I was always starving when we went skiing. My mother said it was the mountain air and the exercise. Soon enough there appeared a small chalet and we could see the smoke from the chimney circling above. Armin skied down to the door and we followed. We took off our skis and began stomping the snow off our ski boots to clean them before entering. It was a small place but the hostess was ready to serve us lunch. It was certainly not a restaurant. We did not order off of a menu. We ate whatever the hostess was serving. It was also the start of the drinking for the adults. They had beer and schnapps and I had a soda called Orange Fanta. That was my favorite drink back then.

After lunch we set off again. Periodically my father and Armin would stop for a sip from a flask. My father would loudly shout, "Kup-Chi Buddha!" and toast Armin who would toast him back. I don't think Armin had a clue what my father was saying. My father was speaking Lao. He was saying, "Thank you Buddha!" After a few stops, Armin started saying it with my father. It was pretty funny to watch. Of course, the more they drank, the more they had to stop, especially when the mountain started to get very steep and craggy.

I'll never forget one section of the mountain when we were standing on a ledge and looking straight down. Armin nodded when we all looked at him in horror. Yep, that's where we were going. Straight down. I gulped. Armin set out and went very, very slowly making wide turns and stopping to check our progress. There were no "Kup-chi Buddha" stops on this part. We all had to concentrate very hard on not falling. If you did, you would end up rolling down the steep, slippery slope and very possibly sustain an injury.

Finally we made it down the hardest part and were close to the bottom of the mountain. The day had flown by. It was already dusk when we reached the van. We were all exhausted. Skiing all day without really stopping is great exercise and challenges the strength and muscles of the legs. At the ski resorts, you ski – then stop – wait in line and catch a lift. That is a pretty long break. Skiing down one huge mountain all day long with few stops is really an accomplishment!

And the adventure was not even over. We still had the drive home! We stopped for dinner where the adults again indulged themselves with imbibing alcohol while I guzzled down another orange Fanta. Armin's brother (our driver and designated sober one), had coffee. Things were starting to get pretty rowdy with Armin, my parents and the other couple all telling stories and laughing it up.

We left the restaurant only to have Armin and my father demand that we stop at another 'watering hole.' We stopped again and this time my father told everyone to "ante up" whatever money they had left. A large stack of bills and coins appeared. After ordering another Fanta for me (thank goodness my mother remembered I was there), a coffee for Armin's brother (I wondered if he was getting as sick of coffee as I was of orange Fanta), my father told the waitress to bring them as much schnapps as the money they had would buy. Everyone thought this was really funny until the waitress came back with four *gigantic* carafes of schnapps and 5 glasses. These carafes were filled to the brim with the clear alcohol. There were gasps of surprise around the table followed by howls of laughter. My mother was laughing so hard she had tears in her eyes. And, do you know, by the time we got ready to leave, those carafes were empty and

Armin's brother and I were the only ones who could walk in a straight line.

Now the really tricky part was that we had to cross the border back into Austria. The Dutchman with us was having so much fun he decided to sing for us. And sing he did. Pretty soon my father and Armin tried to join him. I can still recall the song they sang in their thick, drunken voices: *"Cigarettes and whisky and fine, fine women, they'll drive you crazy, they'll drive you insane."* But the song coming out of their mouths was a slurred version and it sounded like this: *"Ceegareets an' whiskey an' fine fine weemen, dey drives yous crazy dey drives yous insane."* The last word was dragged out so it sounded like, *"Insaaayyyynnnneee."* And they sang it over and over and *over*.

This was all happening as we drove up to the border, which was patrolled by armed guards with machine guns. We had to show our passports as before, however – *unlike* before – the van was now filled with a bunch of roaring drunks, singing and laughing like a group of loonies from the insane asylum. The guard stopped us with an impatient wave.

As soon as the van stopped, quick as a wink (which was surprising since he was so drunk) the Dutchman, still singing, exited the van and began to perform a dance, singing the "Cigarettes and Whiskey" song at the top of his lungs. The Dutchman lurched about, swaying back and forth while Armin and my father howled with laughter. Armin's brother got off the van and started talking to the grinning guards (more had come out of the guard building to see what the ruckus was all about). Apparently Armin's brother knew a few of the guards and after a brief explanation, they viewed the spectacle before them with good humor – fortunately for all of us.

I could see my mother was looking worried but the guards finally waved the Dutchman and Armin's brother back onto the van. The Dutchman was so far gone by then he had to crawl into the van and he was *still* singing! My mother and I heaved great sighs of relief when we were allowed to drive off and cross the border into Austria. I can just imagine what would have happened if they had decided not to let us go and dragged my father off for interrogation.

I think Armin's brother was as anxious as I to get home and have everyone still in one piece, because he drove like a madman for a while until, through bleary eyes, my father and Armin insisted they had just seen another bar and wanted to stop. Armin's brother told them it was not a bar. We had just passed through a very small, rural town and even if there was a bar or restaurant, it would certainly be closed at this hour. My father and Armin kept at him and finally Armin's brother gave up and turned around. He stopped in front of the building they were drunkenly pointing at and let them out.

My father and Armin went running to the front door, yelling, "Kup-chi Buddha! We need a drink!" Reluctantly, my mother followed them until she got near the front door which the two men had just burst through with raucous enthusiasm. My mother stopped in her tracks and started shaking her head. I got out of the van to see what she was looking at. As I reached the door, I realized my father and Armin had just barged into a barn filled with cows. The two of them were hanging onto each other, howling with drunken laughter. Well, they were looking for something to drink but I don't think it was milk they were after!

Arriving back at our hotel was a relief. My mother collected the sleeping twins from their caretaker and we went to bed. It was an incredible experience with lots of adventure and humor. After that, though, I was not able to drink orange Fanta for a very long time.

My Sisters, Michelle in front, Diana in back & I am in the middle

Growing Up

I WAS in the eighth grade when I entered the American School of Paris. I rarely saw my sisters at school except on the school bus in the mornings and afternoons. I remember I had to take biology and hated that class, especially when we had to dissect things like a live frog and a real cow's heart. I refused to touch any of the "gross" things with my hands and used to get in trouble for my stubbornness. I thought I would hate science all my life until I took chemistry and loved it.

In eighth grade I fell madly in love with a boy named Mike Costa who never noticed me at all. Even when I went to the dances and followed his movements with my big, mooning eyes, he never once asked me to dance. I think he had a girlfriend but I don't remember for sure. All I know is it was my first experience with thwarted love.

I also had my first experience with what it must be like to be "stalked." There were two boys in my class who were identical twins. They were thin with dark hair and very pale complexions. They acted extremely strange and had no friends. For whatever reason, they fixated on me and followed me around school. It was unnerving because I would try to avoid one of them only to run smack into the other one. They never spoke to me, just watched me all the time. I never told anyone about my fear.

One time I was in the stairwell and I saw one of them at the top of the stairs and the other waiting for me at the bottom. That scared me. I felt trapped. I ran down the stairs and raced by, trying to avoid the dark eyes that were watching me silently. Eventually they left me alone but I never forgot that awful feeling.

I tried out to be a junior cheerleader and made the team. I was gloriously happy. I always got to be "on top" of the pyramid routines because I was small and could jump high. I loved wearing my cheerleading uniform on game days. We took our role in supporting our basketball and rugby teams seriously. Our routines were not complex or intricately difficult; they were simple, fun to do and our cheers were genuine.

We traveled all over Europe with the teams. We would stay with other American families in the different countries while our teams played against the other American schools. We felt like we were an important part of the whole process. When I came back to the United States I was so disillusioned by the cheerleaders I saw and the whole complicated process of trying out for the squad. It seemed to me that the girls were phony and full of themselves. Makeup, clothes and status were more important than whether teams lost or won. Of course, my whole transition back into the U.S. was a very difficult one – but that story comes later.

I used to make my sisters come to my room and watch me practice my routines. My poor sisters. I could make them do anything I wanted. All I had to do was promise to play a game with them and they were "mine." One time, I was up in my room reading and eating an apple. When I finished, I had the apple core but I did not feel like going all the way down to the kitchen to throw it away (one of my mother's adamant rules was that we could not throw away food in our rooms). So, I called and called to my sisters. It was Michelle who wearily climbed the three flights of stairs to come and see what I wanted. I held out the apple core and said, "Can you throw this away for me?" Sighing, she took it and did what I asked. Hard to believe but true. Even my sisters admit it. That would certainly *not* happen today, I assure you!

My first experience with dating was in the ninth grade. I had a "real" boyfriend and his name was Darren Hillicoss. I was so in love. I believe it is true when they say you never forget your first love. I can still picture him in my head. I dated him exclusively for three years – even after returning to the United States.

Darren was tall and blond with a solid build. My parents were not too impressed with my choice of beau. I think they felt he was "beneath me" because he was not very intelligent or ambitious. I remember my first "date" with Darren. He asked me to meet him in the city (Paris) to go to a movie at one of the theatres on the Champs Elysses. I don't even remember the movie because I was so nervous and excited about going on a *real* date. We went to an afternoon feature because my parents did not want me in the city after dark.

My father was to pick me up after the movie. My father was running late so Darren and I stood around a bit awkwardly. Finally I saw my father's car. He pulled up to the curb, jumped out and said loudly, "Well, now, *where the hell* have you been? Screwing around again?!?"

I knew my father was just joking. Exasperated, I said, "*Dad!*" and looked over at Darren who had visibly paled, thinking my father was really angry.

"Hi. Jack Platt's the name. How are you?" My father stuck his hand out.

Darren – whom I believe was now shaking in fear – said in a trembling voice, "Fine, sir." He shook my father's hand quickly, moved back and began a jerky half-run, half-walk down the sidewalk. The word, "Bye!" was yelled over his shoulder as an afterthought.

My father looked at me and shrugged a question. I rolled my eyes at him and got in the car. "Dad. I think you scared him to death!" I exclaimed. "He'll probably never look at me again."

"Gosh, I'm sorry, honey." My father said, trying to look suitably chastised although I could he was fighting a smile. "He'll be fine. Don't you worry." I sighed. This was typical behavior by my father. He was off the hook when I found out Darren was still interested in dating me. My father's outrageous behavior is legend in our family.

Prom night in Paris for Darren & I

Darren lived with his younger brother, father and stepmother in an apartment in Paris. He loved his father but had difficulties getting along with his new stepmother who was quite young. When I first met her, my initial impression was that she was very snobbish. Turned out I was right. She was tall and thin with boy-short black hair. This made her narrow, thin face appear drawn and gaunt. She wore flashy clothes and lots of jewelry. Darren and Michael were often angry with their father because he spent so much money on this woman. While she had a new outfit almost weekly,

Michael was wearing hand-me downs from Darren. After I was exposed more and more to the family dynamics, I thought it was pathetic to see their father doting on such a self-centered woman.

My parents' introduction to the stepmother was both unexpected and disastrous. My aunt Polly, her husband (Big Tony), my cousins (Antonia and Sashy), and our old friend, Fred, had come to see us for the Christmas holidays. While they were visiting, Darren asked me on a date to go and see the movie *Carrie* in the city. That turned out to be a BIG mistake. The movie scared me to death and I was so frightened I could not take the train back to the house by myself. Poor Darren. Not knowing what else to do, he accompanied me home.

Everyone had gone out to dinner so the house was empty when we arrived. Darren decided to call his father and ask him to come and pick him up. The problem was that Darren ended up talking to his stepmother who demanded to know why he was calling. When she found out, she chewed him out. He was almost in tears when he got off the phone but said she was coming to get him. Since she had to drive out from the city, it would be a while before she would arrive. In the meantime, I just sat on the sofa with Darren. I was scared to even go upstairs to my room by myself.

My parents soon arrived back from dinner. After hearing my explanation of why Darren was there and taking one look at my face, my father told Darren he appreciated what he had done. We also explained about the stepmother coming to pick him up. Boy, were we in for a treat when she arrived. Big Tony and my father together are a riot and if you add in the element of Fred, the three of them can be quite devilish.

We heard a knock on the door. My father opened the front door and in walked the stepmother. She was carrying a helmet and was dressed from head to toe in a black leather motorcycle outfit. She had ridden her motorcycle to pick Darren up. She obviously felt she was looking very sexy because – as she was introduced around – she was obviously trying to flirt with all the men and my mother and my aunt were sitting right there! Darren looked horribly embarrassed and kept trying to get her to go – but my wicked father offered her a drink. My heart sank when she girlishly accepted. This was when it got dangerous. My father, Big Tony and Fred had all been drinking already and they could smell blood – and this was not an intelligent woman.

They started asking her questions about the motorcycle, the outfit and what she did with all the chains that were all over her outfit. She thought they were genuinely interested. She never once caught on to the fact that they were making fun of her. Finally, after she realized she was really not welcome, she left in a huff with Darren following. He had his head down and was red-faced with embarrassment. I watched as she started yelling at him at the gate and I felt bad. He'd done the right thing and was now being punished for it.

The older I got, the more I discovered the freedom of living in Europe. The public transportation system is far more sophisticated and far-reaching than in the United States. By the 10th grade, I had a group of close-knit friends. We used to go to the city and catch a movie in the late afternoon or early evening.

My close group of friends at the American School of Paris.
(I am 2ⁿᵈ from the left)

Most of us lived in different parts of the city or the outlaying towns (like I did) and so we all took public transportation. I had to take a train to the "Gard de Nord," which was the North train station in Paris. Then I caught the metro to wherever we were meeting in the city. The freedom of being able to get around without having to ask my parents to drive me or pick me up was wonderful.

I learned that there were a few drawbacks, however. One of the first and most noticeable was that the French (and actually most Europeans) have no concept of "personal space*." In the United States, we have a very large personal space. Usually, when Americans are around strangers or in a strange place, they prefer to keep as much space between

---

* Personal space is the space immediately around you that you claim as your own. It is an invisible volume of space, sort of like a space-suit that you wear; it's close to you at the back, a little wider at the sides, and bigger in front. When people enter this space, you may feel uncomfortable. The size of your personal space can change, depending on whom you're with, where you are and what culture you are from.

themselves and those around them. The French are the opposite.

For example, if I got on a train in the United States and there was one other person in the compartment, I would find a seat far away from that person. In France, the exact opposite happens. Even if there is only *one* person sitting in the compartment, the next person who boards the train will come and sit *right* next to them.

I found out about the "lack of personal space" one evening when I was riding the train home after a movie. I was sitting contentedly in the vacant compartment when the train stopped and in stepped a Frenchman. I only barely glanced at him and then continued to read my book. Sure enough, the dark-haired, large man slowly walked down the isle, ignoring all the many empty seats and sat down *right next to me!* This was one of the most uncomfortable situations I have found myself in. Not only was the man heavy and overweight - his overcoat buttons straining at the abdomen - but he also smelled terrible, like he had not washed recently. The whole situation definitely started to freak me out but I just sat there, not really knowing what to do.

At the very next station, as soon as the train rolled to a stop, I got off and ran to the head of the train where I knew the conductor was supposed to be. To my relief, the conductor was there. I found a seat close by. After that experience, I always got on the first compartment at night and chose a seat near the train operator. I did not relish the thought of a large, smelly man sitting next to me again.

Unfortunately, there are situations in every part of the world where we need to use our common sense to protect ourselves. The most frightening thing that ever happened to me on the streets in Paris was one night when a friend, Emily, and I had gone to the city to see a movie and she was coming home with me to spend the night. When we got on the train at the North station, I noticed an unshaven, badly dressed man get on behind us. He sat quite close to where we were sitting. After awhile, I forgot about him.

During the ride home, Emily and I talked and whispered our secrets as two young girls do. When we got to Vaucresson, I noticed that the train was almost completely empty except for the homeless-looking man. As we exited the station, I saw the man had also gotten off the train. This worried me and I urged Emily to hurry as it was dark and we still had to get up the hill using the shortcut and go down the couple of blocks to my house. The train station was well lit but the roads in Vaucresson had very few lights. In fact, it was almost completely dark taking the shortcut. I kept looking back but I did not see the man. I kept going at a fast pace, anxious to get home.

Finally we reached my street and had only a few blocks to walk. We were both breathing pretty heavily from our efforts. Suddenly I sensed the man behind us. He was still not that close but I told Emily that there was a man behind us. She turned, alarmed, and looked at me with a question in her eyes about what we should do.

My initial instinct was to run but then I recalled all the warnings I got when we were in Laos about not running from any stray dogs because that could cause a dog to attack. In some strange way, I equated this man to a rabid dog and I thought that running away would provoke him. I just told Emily to keep walking faster. I could see the gate to our house up ahead and I told Emily we were almost there when out of the corner of my eye I saw the man reaching for Emily's shoulder. I screamed and yelled at her to "*RUN!*" and began running myself. The man also started running but he was slow and unsteady on his feet. I reached the gate, gasping and terrified. I grabbed Emily, pulled her in and closed the gate. "Run to the house!" I yelled. I was hot on her tail when I turned and saw the man peering through the gate.

We dashed up the steps, pushed open the front door and slammed it shut. We stood in the hall, gasping for breath. I felt immense relief flood me as I realized we were safe. Both my parents had heard the ruckus (the door slamming which was a "no-no") and asked us what was wrong. I made the story as brief as possible, saying only that a man had appeared on the sidewalk and had gotten so close that he alarmed us and we ran. I told my parents we had probably scared ourselves to death for nothing.

I left out the part that he followed us all the way from the North train station in the city. Again I was afraid I would not be allowed my freedom. My father walked to the gate and looked up and down the street but saw nothing. We were very lucky. I was much more cautious about being alone in the dark on the streets after that.

My Farewell from Paris

AT THE end of my father's tour, we moved out of our house and into a hotel for our final two weeks in Paris. I was having a difficult time accepting that we were really moving back to the United States. I was sixteen and enjoying my independence. I had many friends and a boyfriend whom I adored so the thought of leaving made me despondent. It may be for this reason that I was distracted and not paying attention on one particular spring day in downtown Paris.

I had just gotten off the metro and was headed for our hotel. There was a great deal of traffic because it was close to lunchtime. I hurried down the sidewalk. Without bothering to look, I darted out between two parked cars, planning to run across the street to the hotel and was hit by a taxicab. One moment I was on my feet then – *BOOM* – the next minute I was flying through the air.

Fortunately for me, the traffic was so congested that the taxi had not been moving very fast. I landed on my side and rolled onto my back, dazed and gasping for the air that had been knocked out of my chest. The taxi driver and another person suddenly appeared above me and after seeing that my eyes were open, started jabbering questions in French. I opened my mouth to tell them I was okay, but no sound would come out.

In typical French fashion, the taxi driver and the other person started arguing – perhaps about who was at fault – and as I gingerly sat up, it appeared as if they'd forgotten I was even there. Their voices got louder and louder as did their arm gestures. A crowd began to gather, watching the spectacle. I shook my head and tried to stand up, resting my arm on the hood of the car that hit me. Feeling sick, confused and – at this point – invisible, I staggered away, dragging my left leg behind me, which was now screaming in pain and focused on getting to the hotel. My whole thought process had switched to survival-mode and I just wanted my mother. I reached the hotel before the men realized I had left and they started running after me. I panicked. I tried to move quicker, crying out in pain and began literally to crawl up the hotel stairs. The elevator was out of order and our hotel room was on the 3rd floor.

I finally made it to our door and started screaming for my mother. She opened the door and I fell into her arms while she kept asking me what was wrong. She says that my face was chalk-white and I was shaking like a leaf. Not knowing what else to do, she sat me down on the bed and ran a bath. Whenever something bad happened to my sisters or me – like we had a bad fall or a bike accident – my mother always put us in a hot bath to soothe the body and dry the tears. To this day, whenever something bad happens to me (like the time I ran my husband's brand new fire-engine-red Mustang into the garage door), I run myself a hot bath to ease my nerves and soul. It really works.

The injury I sustained from being hit by the taxi was a gigantic contusion to my upper left thigh. Although painful, it was not life threatening. I limped for several weeks but the swelling and tenderness soon disappeared. The only reminisces of the accident were my vivid dreams that reoccurred for many years. I am thankful that is all that is left. That was my farewell from Paris, the City of Love.

Diana, Doris (my mother-in-law), Michelle, Randy, me & Mom

Return to the U.S.A. 1977

My Dad & me

Epilogue

MY RETURN to the United States was the most difficult move I ever made. During my years of living overseas, I had discovered that I was a very social person and had a way of making friends easily. Back in the U.S., however, I soon began to doubt myself completely. I was not prepared for the hostility and coldness of my peers.

It is sad to say that for the first three months at Rockville High School, not a single person – other than the teachers and administrators – spoke to me or even tried to find out who I was. I tried to talk to other kids but was rebuffed over and over again. I could not believe how cruel and vindictive the kids were. The girls laughed at me behind my back and pointed at my "weird" clothes. I tried to fit in as best I could. I begged my mother to take me shopping so I could find the "right" clothes to wear, but that did nothing to stop the jeering and snide remarks. I was miserable, lonely and missed my friends in France terribly.

Amazingly, the first person to actually speak to me was a boy named Mike O'Connor who was in my Driver's Education class. He was the class clown and very popular. He was good-looking with dark wavy hair and dark brown eyes. He was fascinated that I was a junior and taking Physics – he saw me reading my physics book in class. He wanted to know if I was some kind of genius (apparently it was unusual for a junior to be taking senior-level and college-preparation classes). I told him I had gone to school overseas and had already taken all the other science classes. Although he did not talk to me every time we had class together, sometimes he would sit down and ask a question or two. The other students just stared.

After the first semester of my junior year, Mike and I wound up in the same gym class. The teacher announced we were going to have a co-ed badminton tournament and partners had to be from the opposite sex. I sighed when I heard this because that meant we would have to pick partners and – as usual – no one would pick me.

To my utter surprise, Mike walked over and asked if I would partner with him. I was shocked and tried to say yes but no words would come out of my mouth so I just nodded affirmatively. I felt laser-sharp nasty stares from the other girls. Later I found out that he instantly regretted his impulsive invitation because he wanted to *win* and he had no idea if I was any good. Much to his delight, I was an excellent player and we won the tournament.

After that, Mike was smitten and asked me out. It is sad to say that things got better for me because we were dating, but it's true. Because "Mr. Popular" was interested in me, people finally started talking to me. But I will never forget my re-introduction to the United States and the disdainful way I was treated just because I was new.

Life went on and I graduated with *great relief* from Rockville High School. I went from there to the College of William and Mary (after a one-year stint at Rollins College in Florida – but that is another story in itself) and graduated in 1983 with a Bachelor's degree in Economics.

Today I am happily married to a wonderful man – Randy. We live in California with our two beloved cats and I am doing what I love – *writing*.

Randy is holding Cleo (Cleopatra) and I am holding Sammy (Samurai)
October 2003

<u>*The End for Now*</u>